Praise for *Reader of Hearts*

"A fun read."

— Caroline Myss, author of
Anatomy of the Spirit and *Sacred Contracts*

"With humor and humility
and practical everyday advice,
Darrin Owens will take you
into the soul of the mystical experience."

— Denise Linn,
author of *Sacred Space*

"Astral, magical, and miracle —
Darrin Owens is a force of psychic talent,
and it shows in this wonderful book
of story and spiritual exercises."

— Jane Olivor, Academy Award–nominated
recording artist

"Darrin Owens has distilled a wealth of experience
onto the pages of this book. I highly recommend
Reader of Hearts to those wanting to tap into
a deeper understanding of their psychic nature."

— Susan Taylor, PhD, nutritional biochemist
and producer of *The Vital Energy Program* audio course

READER
of HEARTS

READER *of* HEARTS

THE LIFE AND TEACHINGS
OF A RELUCTANT PSYCHIC

DARRIN OWENS

FINDHORN
Press

Published by Findhorn Press
305a The Park
Forres IV36 3TE

Text design and typography by Tona Pearce Myers

British Library Cataloguing-in-Publication Data:
A catalogue record for this book is available from the British Library.

First printing, April 2006
ISBN-10: 1-84409-046-9
ISBN-13: 978-1-84409-046-4

Printed in Canada on partially recycled, acid-free paper

10   9   8   7   6   5   4   3   2   1

This book is dedicated to
Carol J,
Carol S,
Jane,
Angela,
Dolores,
and
Mom

CONTENTS

Chapter 2: The Sevenfold Path of Spiritual Growth   35

Chapter 3: Spiritual Awakening   42

Chapter 4: Divine Darkness   53

Chapter 5: Interior Power and Sacred Energy   61

Chapter 6: Inner Attunement   72

Chapter 7: Conscious Creation   87

Chapter 8: Wholistic Living   97

Chapter 9: Oneness   109

Conclusion: The Journey Continues   120

PREFACE

*A*fter working for more than ten years on the spiritual and holistic healing circuit, or what I sometimes call "spiritual Hollywood," I became weary of seeing all the metaphysical nonsense that passes for spiritual wisdom. I would go to bookstores and see New Age shelves filled with how-to books on being a spiritual healer, a medium, or a psychic, some claiming to have you reading auras in sixty seconds. I met some of the more popular celebrity psychics and teachers and came away convinced that what most of them were offering wasn't much different from a spiritual carnival show. They were like the long-nailed fortune-tellers and glamorized mediums, charging an arm and a leg to tell you what you want to hear, or what they want you to hear.

As a practicing psychic, I have always believed that a true psychic is a spiritual director, not a fortune-teller. *Psychic* means "of the soul." A psychic's true job is to bring people into the present, where the soul resides, not to catapult them into the future with promises of love, money, and success. It is the psychic's role to help people get in touch with divine wisdom — to be the channel for this wisdom and not claim to be its source. How had psychics, I wondered, become providers of cheap entertainment (which, unfortunately, costs a lot of money) for those who are seeking a quick fix? Where did the idea of divine guidance go?

I realized that many psychics, real or self-proclaimed, were just taking advantage of a modern trend. People seem to run to psychics or seminars that promise paranormal activity or immediate answers to all their questions. They want to think that they can gain inner peace by talking to the dead or seeing the future.

One thing I had become certain of in my brief time on this planet was that we cannot learn the science of our souls in its totality by simply looking into the future, chatting with angels or aliens, communicating with those on the other side, learning astral projection, or surrounding ourselves with spiritual or new age paraphernalia. I knew that we needed to stop paying so much attention to what is "out there" and pay more attention to what is within ourselves. I knew that it was time for true, authentic inner practices to take reign and guide us to a better perspective on life and ourselves. I'm not saying that talking to angels or dead loved ones isn't a legitimate process to soul growth — in some cases, it is. What I'm saying is that these paranormal occurrences are just experiences on the path, not the path itself. The path of your soul and its destiny lies only in you, and it's waiting to be discovered by you and no one else.

That's why I decided to write this book.

My hope is that this book will have some power to inspire, to heal, and to guide readers to a better understanding of themselves and the world they live in. I hope that it becomes part of the call for a pure sense of spirituality to arise. I hope that it builds for you the confidence that you already have within you all the answers you need.

I hadn't yet reached thirty years of age when I wrote most of what's in these pages. So, you may be wondering what a spring chicken like me could possibly have to say about the workings of the universe. Though I haven't been around for a long time, I've seen and experienced quite a bit of the unseen world — or as I think of it, the mystical world. I've been able to do this because the Gods gifted me with unusually strong psychic abilities. In doing so, they made it my responsibility to use these abilities to help others navigate their spiritual journeys. They gave me my mission: to teach and express the wisdom I've gained as a psychic.

I never expected or wanted to be a psychic or a teacher of spirituality. Who truly does? When we were kids, did any of us get up in front of the classroom and say, "When I grow up, I want to be a famous psychic"? As a kid I had my heart set on being a singer. I dreamed of singing on stage for sellout audiences at the London Palladium or New York's Carnegie Hall. I was an avid member of the fine arts class in school and performed in all of the variety shows and musical contests I could enter.

But the Gods had a deeper plan for me. I was destined to be, in the words of one of my spiritual teachers, a "reader of hearts." As a reader of hearts, I offer this to you — your personal handbook for the soul.

EVERYDAY MYSTICISM FOR THE TWENTY-FIRST CENTURY

A deeper, more meaningful world exists all around us that we can't perceive directly with our five senses. It's the invisible plane of energy vibrating through the cosmos, the world of magic, the spiritual realm, the all-pervading presence of the divine. This book is about healing our souls by connecting with that world. In short, it's about finding magic in everyday life.

There have always been among us a few gifted people who can, in the blink of an eye, move beyond the physical realm and into the spiritual. With an effortless shift in perception, they see the divine presence in everything. These people are often called mystics. Throughout the centuries, mystics have played an important role in Christianity, Islam, Judaism, Hinduism, and other religious traditions.

Mystics come into this world with a little something extra, but they don't have exclusive rights to the world beyond the senses. Each of us has part of the mystic within us. Even if we can't enter the transcendent dimension as fully or as easily as mystics like Joan of Arc or Francis of Assisi, we can share some aspects of the mystical experience. We all have the ability to see the divine in everything. All we have to do is allow ourselves to trust our intuitive powers and expand our awareness and receptivity. And when we do, our souls are perfectly capable of absorbing the same spiritual truths that mystics gain from unceasing prayer or a lifetime of disciplined meditation in a faraway monastery.

Nothing separates a person from the experience of the divine except a closed mind. By "closed mind," I mean a mind that allows itself to see only the physical world and to use only the intellect. I call this the *1-2-3 way of thinking*. Some people call it linear or rational thought. However you name it, it is closed to the reality of the unseen dimensions that lie waiting to be discovered. Sometimes, of course, we need the 1-2-3 way of thinking, but if it's our only operating mode, we miss much of the beauty and majesty of life.

Inside each of us there is a divine essence, an extension of the divine presence in the universe. It's what we call the soul. By reclaiming our mystical selves — altering our perception from the mortal to the mystical — we can get back in touch with that divine essence. A vast universe of untapped potential and wisdom opens up to us when we make this personal connection with the divine.

But just what is the *divine*? I use the word *divine* to be as inclusive as possible. For many people, the divine is God, pure and simple. For others, the concept of God is limiting. I, for one, believe that the divine has many faces or aspects. That's why I sometimes talk about *the Gods*, plural and personified. And I believe that the divine has a feminine, mothering side that's best described by using the term *the Goddess*. In this book I mostly use such terms as *the divine*, *the divine presence*, and *the universe*, but you can substitute *Love*, *God*, or any other word you like. Choose the face of the divine that fits best with the religious or spiritual orientation you bring to this book.

Reclaiming Mystical Experience

We are living in a world that desperately needs to reclaim the mystical experience of the divine. This need can be seen in the way that people are continually searching for meaning, for a higher purpose. We look for meaning in our relationships, in our careers, and in the organizations we belong to. The one place we forget to look is in ourselves, where the divine essence lives.

The world around us is also suffering from the fact that we have lost touch with mystical experience and the divine. For centuries, our earth has been looked on as something to be conquered and controlled. We have polluted the rivers, the oceans, and the air. We have lost respect for the other life forms that share the earth with us. All this has been made possible only by denying the earth's divine nature and severing the mystical connection that humans have with the earth.

For thousands of years, pagan peoples celebrated the earth's divinity in the form of the Goddess. The Goddess represented the cycles of the seasons, the abundance of nature, and the need to treat the earth and its life with reverence. A balance existed between nature and humanity, based on a mystical understanding of nature. Then that balance was destroyed by the rise of a fear-based God system and the greed and hunger for power that came with it. Fear became the force that told people how to worship and live "religious" lives. The Goddess was banished, cast out as an evil presence.

Since that time, our planet has been ravaged by a windstorm of the shadow side of masculine energy. I truly believe that if we are to create peace and make the world a better place for future generations, we must reconnect with the feminine aspect of the divine — call it Mother Earth or the Goddess, if you will — and have its feminine energy come alive in our hearts, to balance the masculine energy that prevails now and has been prevailing for centuries.

I think we are ever so slowly recovering our lost mystical traits, both as individuals and a society. People are beginning to wake up to the fact that the earth is our home and that it's time to revive this planet, make it what it was meant to be — a beautiful manifestation of the divine.

How can we support this trend and help bring back the mystical life force of this planet? We first must regain the divine within ourselves by learning the way of the mystic. When we've reclaimed our divine natures, we can no longer have the closed hearts and negativity that lead the way in polluting our minds and our planet. We are all lights, and when we gather together, lighting one inner lamp after another, we recharge the earth. We are all brothers and sisters of this divine light, and when we become conscious of this, we will revive the life force of our planet.

The Mortal Mind and the Mystical Mind

We are thinking all the time. The question is, Are we thinking with fear or with love? At times we all feel as if we are two people in one. We may think love and light until someone makes us angry, and then a different self takes over and starts contemplating a good old-fashioned tar and feather. Why? We each have access to two ways of being — one guided by the mystical mind and the other ruled by the mortal mind. The mortal mind is the ego, rationality, and the unconscious, whereas the mystical mind is consciousness of the higher self as a manifestation of the divine. A large part of learning the way of the mystic is recognizing the latent aspects of the mystical mind (love) and loosening the ties of the mortal mind (fear).

The mortal mind is stuck in the world of the physical senses; the mystical mind operates apart from your sensory perceptions. In a psycho-spiritual sense, the mystical mind allows you unlimited impressions and intuitions and infuses you with the divine. It's responsible for those *aha*! moments when you know you have been downloaded with wisdom, when you finally get it.

Having a mystical mind and experiencing the mystical world costs nothing; it asks only for your attention and intention. Like Dorothy in *The Wizard of Oz*, the person who wants to be guided by the mystical mind only needs to ask the magic question, "Is there somewhere over the rainbow, somewhere that's better?" Ask that question with serious intent, and you are swept up to a world where everything is in color, where you get to follow a yellow-brick road wearing some flashy ruby slippers.

Now, just because you land in Oz doesn't mean you're

given all the answers. Like Dorothy, you must still seek the truth all the time. Your mortal mind, working from fear, may want a map for the journey, but no map exists. The Gods don't give us maps; they give us guidance.

If you had a map for every situation in life, you would not learn the lessons of experience. You would be more concerned with the destination than the journey. The mystical mind is comfortable living with mystery, knowing that sometimes you just need to be — to surrender to divine guidance and not figure anything out. The mortal mind tends to get us stuck in life by refusing to live in mystery, by always wanting to have the answer, now.

As you gain spiritual wisdom, you will begin to recognize the times when your mortal mind is speaking the loudest and overpowering your mystical mind. By developing this consciousness, you can learn to balance the two and create one mind of harmonious, mystical intelligence.

Wisdom and Knowledge

We gain knowledge from reading books and going to workshops; we gain wisdom from putting that knowledge to use, from experiencing it. For example, you could spend a lifetime reading about creating your own reality, but what good would knowledge of this powerful spiritual truth be if you didn't put it into practice? The truth would just float around in your mind; you could think about it, visualize it, analyze it — but until you live that truth, it doesn't work for you.

Knowledge is an attribute of the mind, and wisdom is an attribute of the soul. As far as the soul is concerned, knowledge without wisdom is useless. The good thing is that the universe will always bring you situations that allow you to practice what you have been reading or learning about — opportunities to transform knowledge into wisdom and nourish your soul. If you don't pay attention to these opportunities, the universe will keep working with you until you do. The universe has all the time in the world.

Saints and mystics through the years have known about the importance of wisdom and have lived their lives accordingly. They have taught their students the spiritual truths, knowing full well that the students would have to experience the lessons to transform knowledge of the truths into wisdom. Christ said, "You can do as I can do," and sent his students out into the world, not only to teach his truth, but also to experience it for themselves. We have several chances to screw up in life until we get it right. When we learn to access the wisdom of life, we rise a little higher toward fulfilling our destinies.

What's to Come

You know that I'm a psychic — but I've been talking about mysticism. So by now you may be wondering, "What does a psychic know about mysticism?" It's true that psychics and mystics are different, but — especially in my case — there's some overlap.

Psychics are able to tap into the mental energy of other people. Through this connection we can know a person's thoughts and emotions and what he or she has experienced in life. But this is really a connection to the person's divine essence, which is a manifestation of the divine energy of the universe, or God. That's why psychics can know something of a person's destiny; it's also why we can communicate with people from a person's past who are now "on the other side." What psychics and mystics share is this connection with the unseen world of the divine. Psychics connect through people; mystics do it directly. For both, the experience of the divine is personal and subjective — and a source of wisdom.

So, even though it would be a stretch for me to call myself a true mystic, I've had wisdom-building mystical experiences. On top of that, I've focused on using my psychic abilities not to tell people what the future holds for them but to give them spiritual guidance. I've been doing what mystics do — using the insights gained from contact with the divine — to teach people about tending to their souls.

I've been a psychic and spiritual director long enough to know about common spiritual blockages and the ways people can overcome them. I've learned about quieting the voices of fear and building inner strength. My clients have given me countless opportunities to work on my own issues, and I've spent lots of time "walking my talk."

Through it all, I've realized that the power to develop spiritually, to strengthen the inner self, comes from a stronger connection to the divine. That's why I've been talking about *everyday mysticism*. I believe the key to it all is learning the mystic's ability to see the divine in everything and eliminate what separates you from it.

That's the basic idea. How to do it, and how to apply it in your spiritual growth, is the subject of this book. I've gathered together the spiritual wisdom I've gained over the years and distilled it into seven different topics. Each topic makes up a separate chapter. These are not lessons on how to become more psychic or how to talk to your spirit guides. They are for tuning and strengthening your inner dynamics. They are meant to help you take more responsibility for your life and spiritual development.

Before I launch into these seven elements of spiritual wisdom, I want to share with you the story of my own spiritual journey, in the hope that it will spark something deeper and more meaningful in your own life. My story has some unusual aspects, as you might expect, but I've gone through the same spiritual passages that other people are likely to experience. And what I've learned along the way is the basis for much of what I offer you in the rest of the book.

Anyway, the Gods have made it clear that they want me to share my story, so here goes.

CHAPTER ONE

A Psychic's Mystic Journey

s I was preparing to make my entrance into the world, my mother wasn't in the best of health. The doctors told her that I might not survive. Even then I didn't like people assuming things about me, so on December 13, 1975, I popped out, very much alive but with the umbilical cord wrapped around my neck three times. They called me the "magic" kid, and my mother named me Darrin, after the husband of the witch on the sixties TV sitcom *Bewitched*. So, certain expectations were placed on me from the very beginning. I grew up loving anything to do with magic. I loved reading stories of wizards, witches, and journeys to mystical faraway lands. *The Wizard of Oz* was a particular favorite, and being a daydreamer, I often wished a twister would come sweep me away from the small Arkansas town I was raised in.

As a kid I had an active imagination — or so my parents

thought when they saw me talking to my invisible friends. I was always having conversations with the thin air. Although I *was* very imaginative, my parents had little idea that my invisible friends were as real as they were. Every child talks to angels, fairies, and spirit guides, but my behavior was probably a little unsettling to my parents.

Or at least to my father, who had no time at all for what he saw as make-believe. He didn't know what to do with me, so he did nothing. He just looked at me as if to say, "What the hell is up with this kid? Whatever it is, it's not from my side of the family." My mother, however, knew there was something special about me that needed protecting. I was a sensitive type and kept to myself — totally different from my two older brothers, who were into sports and fast cars. My mother never told me to stop "making things up" or that I should "get real" and be more like my brothers. She always told me to listen with my heart and it would be okay. I was lucky to have had a least one open-minded parent.

Word spread to family and friends that I was a bit on the odd side. Around the tender age of three, my mom would plop me down in the yard while she hung clothes out to dry. Rabbits, squirrels, and even deer would walk right up to me and allow me to pet them. It happened so regularly that my uncle said he wanted to camp out in the bushes surrounding our yard to go hunting. Needless to say, my mom didn't allow it.

One morning, at the age of seven, I walked out to the patio and saw hummingbirds in our morning-glory vine. I sat and watched the birds dart here and there for hours. At one point, I walked over to the vine and held out my hand, and a purple and green hummingbird alighted on it. I remember it like it was yesterday. I sat on the ground while the peaceful little thing let me pet it. Its feathers were like silk, and I could feel its tiny heart beat. My older brother drove up, and seeing me sitting there surrounded by hummingbirds, he shouted, "Holy shit, he's freakin' Snow White!"

I can remember being able to feel things very strongly. I would look at a person, and all of these images would flood through my mind. I would know his or her feelings, desires, and intentions, the general workings of that person's life. Eventually I learned to control this ability and turn the juice on or off when need be. But it took me a long time to realize that it wasn't normal to receive psychic impressions. I thought everyone felt and sensed things like I did.

When I turned nine, my father left and never returned. Mom had to work many hours while raising me alone. This is when I learned what it meant to struggle in life. I used to say that mom and I were so poor the ants felt sorry for us and brought back the food they took.

Mom thought it would do us both good to start going to church. I liked that idea. I loved the thought of gathering with folks who loved God. But after a few months of revivals and Sunday school, I found myself more worried about ditching hell after death than loving God. And to make matters worse, the more I attended church, the more I became convinced that my mysterious feelings and abilities were powers given to me by the Devil himself.

I feared for my life every day, thinking that God would catch on to me and the Devil would come in the night to take me away to burn in hell forever. I tried to be a good Christian lad, but the church teachings didn't sit well with me. I didn't understand how God could be vengeful like the minister kept talking about. I hadn't been afraid of God before going to church.

Somewhere, I had wandered off my yellow-brick road. My confusion and fears built a wall around me, and a cloud of depression set in. Fully into this spiritual crisis I began to enter puberty. Amid the emotional turmoil, my psychic abilities seemed to skyrocket. I could hear thoughts and voices, and I saw lights flashing here and there, in and around everything. It was harder for me to control my sensitivity than it had ever been before. I thought I was getting a brain tumor. My mother took me to a doctor for tests. They couldn't find anything wrong. Before long, I was depressed all the time and didn't leave the house except to go to school or church. I stayed indoors and read or watched television. I felt safe at home, with no crazy energies flying around me.

To try to cope with all of this I began to listen to music religiously. Music could take me out of my body for a while and into a whole new world. I loved strong female voices, still do. I listened to Judy Garland, Edith Piaf, Billie Holiday, and Patsy Cline. They sang with great emotion, which helped me create an inner emotional outlet.

I had no spiritual mentor or paranormal investigator to tell me what was really going on with me. I could not go to the local minister for fear of being burned at the stake. I had already been baptized so many times to wash my sins away that I was growing gills. I was sent to a psychiatrist; his conclusion was that I was perfectly normal and just needed a boost in the social-skills category. He wanted to put me on drugs, but Mom and I both said no.

My Spiritual Awakening

I remember lying on my bed one night at the age of fifteen. I asked God or whoever was running the show for help. I wanted to know why I was here and what my life was about. I wanted to love God the way I had as a child. I wanted that magical part of myself to return. I wanted to feel safe again. All I could hear back from the universe were the crickets in the night. So I continued with my ultimatum to God: *Listen, God. I have had it. I don't know what's going on. I don't know what to believe anymore. Is there something you want from me? Why am I different? Why do these weird things happen to me? Am I bound for damnation as I've been told? Here's the deal: either you show me your truth or I'm outta here. If I'm heading for hell, it won't be much different than what I'm living now, just hotter. I mean it, God: I'm going to kill myself tomorrow night, so you have one day to show me your truth! Amen! And good night!*

I went to bed that night angrier than I'd ever been. Before finally falling asleep, I planned out how I would do myself in the next night. I was queasy at the sight of blood, so slicing my wrist was a bad idea and way too messy. I would take an overdose of pills.

When I got up the next morning, Mom had already left for work. I'm sure if she had heard my talk with God the night before, she would have stayed home. It was a Saturday, so I decided, for some odd reason, that I would rent a movie.

I went to our local grocery store, where they had just put in a small rent-a-video section. I scanned the shelves, wondering what would be a good film for my last day of life — maybe *Mommie Dearest*? No, that wouldn't do. Nothing seemed like the right thing to watch, and that made me feel even more frustrated with life. Just as I was about to give up and leave, I noticed a video sitting by itself, and I picked it up. It was *Out on a Limb*, Shirley MacLaine's film about her spiritual quest and search for truth. I already knew about Shirley; the preacher at my church did a whole sermon on the New Age and said Shirley was the leader of a destructive cult movement. *Well*, I thought, *all the more reason for me to watch it.*

I took it home and popped it into the VCR. I barely remember the experience of watching it. I was in a trance-like state through the whole thing. I do remember this: when the movie was over, I knew that God had done what I had demanded — I had been shown the truth. There was much more to explore, and my exploration would begin with the journey into myself. I knew I had to take a leap of faith, like Shirley, and become the seeker.

Finding My Inner Power

Suddenly, I was feeling great. I had something to look forward to when I got out of bed every day. I felt like a wide-eyed kid on Christmas morning. And the better I felt about myself, the more I began to relax on the inside and not be so afraid. I came to know in my heart that there was an all-loving divine force supporting me. I had watched a psychic on television talk about protecting yourself with the white light of the Holy Spirit. So, every day I got out of bed and wrapped this light around me. It worked. My empathic connections with people felt more manageable, and my psychic chaos began to taper off.

I began to feel better at school as well. I joined the choir and began singing in variety shows and local talent contests. I finally felt I was claiming my voice (literally and spiritually) and I could walk out on a stage and sing about it. There was nothing like feeling the warmth of a spotlight and hearing the roar of applause. It was more than just feeling accepted; it was about expressing emotion and connecting to people. Stage fright was never a problem. A strong energy took over when I performed, the same energy that takes over now when I teach in front of a crowd. The higher part of me stepped in, and the voice of spirit stole the show.

I was bound and determined to know more about the outer limits of my soul, but living in a small town made it a bit difficult to find any books on spirituality not authored by a televangelist. I called my sister-in-law Angela, who lived in Little Rock (the big city), and asked her if she had read any metaphysical books or was interested in otherworldly things. "You bet," she answered. "I'll bring you a stack of books when your brother and I come visit." And she did! Right after they arrived, Angela took me aside and whispered, "Come with me," and we went into my bedroom. "Don't show these to your brother, or we'll both be in for it," she said as she piled five books into my arms. The subjects ranged from reincarnation and ESP to Zen philosophy. My brother David would have popped a lung if he had known his wife was smuggling New Age propaganda to his little brother. David was a strict conservative. He didn't go for any of the New Age wishy-washy ideas at all. Fortunately, even though his little brother was a little on the weird side, David would not have traded me in for the world.

After David and Angela left, I crammed in metaphysics. I would run home after school or choir, lock myself in my room, and read as much as I could, often into the wee hours of the morning. I didn't tell a soul what I was reading. One day, I decided to bring one of my books to school with me so I could read it during study hall. I popped it open and became engrossed — so engrossed that I jumped when my teacher came up and tried to take the book from me. I held onto it and looked up at her with a cold stare. She asked, "Why are you reading this book?" Before I could even begin to answer, she said, "Please tell me you are reading this to be informed about false teachers and Satanic cults." Now, by that point in my spiritual growth I had developed a liberated tongue, and I replied, "No, I'm reading this because I want to learn how to have an out-of-body experience in five minutes." My sarcasm had the intended effect. She gasped and walked straight out of the room.

The next thing I knew, I was being called into the hallway to stand between the teacher and the principal. My by-now very distressed teacher was telling the principal the story of how she had "caught" me reading the book and how she thought an intervention was needed for the sake of my salvation. The principal took the book and in his most minister-like voice said, "Now son, you don't want to be reading far out stuff like this. Your teacher was worried, and she just wanted to help you."

I blurted out, "Help me? How? By shoving her beliefs down my throat?" While part of me said these words, another part wondered where this voice had come from. I had always been the quiet kid in the corner, never causing trouble of any kind. But something had snapped, and now I was this opinionated youth with no fear of telling people what I thought. I had gone through too much at this point to let anyone tell me what my spirituality should be.

I said to my teacher, "Thanks for the concern, but I'm fine with my spirituality."

"Well dear, what religion are you?" she replied. "Aren't you a Christian?"

I replied very sternly, "I'm spiritual," but they didn't seem to understand my answer. Then I said, "This is a public school, am I right?"

"Yes," replied the principal, knowing that I had him in a corner.

"Then, I will read and believe what I want; I'm not hurting anyone and sure not trying to convert anyone." I shot a look at my teacher and waited to see what would happen next. The bell rang, and suddenly it was over, just like that. I shook the principal's hand, nodded at my teacher, took my book back, and walked to my next class.

What the hell was that all about? I thought as I walked down the hall.

In my head I heard the reply: "Your true voice." I stopped in the middle of the hallway, totally excited about acting like Joan Crawford or one of those other big-shouldered broads with attitude. "Don't fuck with me, fellas!" I shouted in my head as I walked purposefully into my next class.

Coming into My Own as a Psychic

A few days after my seventeenth birthday, my mother came home early from work and said she had been let go. She said the time had come for us to leave our little town and move on. That night she had a long talk with my brother David. When she got off the phone, she announced, "Darrin, we're moving to Little Rock." My brother said my mom and I could stay with them until we could find jobs and a place of our own. So, off we went to the big city. It was a dream come true; Little Rock was like the Big Apple to this small-town kid.

It wasn't as hard getting used to big-city life as I thought it would be. I actually fit right in. I enjoyed the fact that I could haunt bookstores with metaphysical books and buy any I could get my hands on. I also had more opportunities to sing. Everything seemed to flow just right.

By now I was getting serious about my singing career. I sang for some people from a record label who had come to town in search of new talent. They loved my performance and wanted me to compete in a contest of finalists two months later. If I won, I could get a record deal. I decided to do it. One day while I was studying sheet music, the mail came, and my brother started going through it. He looked over a mustard-colored flyer, mumbled to himself, "How the hell did this psychic stuff get in here?" and proceeded to toss it into the trash. That night when he went to bed, curiosity got the better of me. I went to the trash can and read the crumpled piece of paper. It was an invitation to the Karen Patterson Spiritual Center. They were having their annual summer solstice gathering the coming weekend and everyone was invited. The flyer went on about the Center's founder, Karen, and how she was a metaphysical teacher and internationally known psychic. Something in me jumped; I knew I had to go to this gathering. I asked myself the same question David had: why had they sent this here? He never did receive anything else from them, and later I found out he wasn't even on their mailing list.

The next morning I showed the flyer to my mother and

asked if we could go. She said yes. I think she really wanted to see what I was getting into. Finally, I thought, I might find a place where I could really get a clue about what was going on in my world.

On Saturday, mom and I followed the directions on the flyer and pulled up to a white house. There were already several cars parked in the lot. As mom found an open parking space, I read the sign on front of the house: KAREN PATTERSON SPIRITUAL CENTER AND THE METAPHYSICAL CHRISTIAN CHURCH. *Wow! This is a church too*, I thought to myself.

We walked in, and it felt safe to me, almost like I was coming to a family reunion. A woman named Ann met us at the door; she was as beautiful as an angel. "Hi. Welcome to the Spiritual Center. Come in. Karen will be here soon and we'll get started." "Get started with what?" my mom whispered to me. Poor Mom — she looked like a fish out of water. I walked into the living room area, and it was crammed with books. They had their own bookstore! I was in Heaven. Subjects ranged from UFOs, past lives, and angels to the lost books of the Bible.

After scanning the bookshelves, I decided to mingle a bit. I'm not a social butterfly, even to this day, but I found myself chatting with other people and learning about their spiritual journeys. I realized I was not alone when it came to a search for a deeper meaning to life. Everyone I talked to had had some kind of mystical experience that propelled them on a spiritual quest. I was really excited to be in a place where like minds gathered.

Karen Patterson was about to begin her talk. People I spoke with told me she was not only a teacher and minister but also a well-known psychic detective and had solved several cases throughout the years. She had just opened the center the year before and started her Metaphysical Christian Church. She and another woman, Franny Butler — who would later become my primary mentor — did psychic consulting on a weekly basis.

We all found our seats, and Karen approached the front of the group. She opened with a prayer and began a talk on the celebration of each season as an initiation for the soul. She went on to discuss the importance of connecting to God in your own personal way. My mother whispered in my ear, "I've never heard this kind of God talk before. I like it!" I smiled at the thought of mom getting to experience the joy I was feeling now.

Afterward, I approached Karen and told her how much I enjoyed her talk and thanked her. She looked at me and said, "Come with me." A look of pure terror appeared on my mom's face as I told her I was going to talk with Karen. She was left to fend for herself among a sea of New Agers and had no clue what her son was about to get into.

Karen showed me to her reading office. I walked in, smelling the woodsy scent of sandalwood in the air. The walls were forest green, and there were plants everywhere. She had me sit on a plushy couch next to her antique red velvet reading chair. Behind her was a statue of the Mother Mary and a picture of Christ, laughing. On the coffee table in front of me was a golden statue of the archangel Michael. *So, this is a psychic's office*, I thought, *and no crystal ball or hanging beads*. I felt right at home.

Karen sat down and pulled out a beaded cigarette case and a lighter. "Mind if I smoke?" she asked.

"Uh, no. My whole family does," I stammered.

"But you don't," she said with a smile.

"No, I don't."

"Good, don't start; it's a nasty habit to get into." And then, after only a moment's pause, she stated matter-of-factly, "So, kiddo, you've had a wild past couple of years. I'm glad you decided to stick around."

My mouth hung open, and all I could do was mutter, "Uh huh... you know?"

"Of course I know. I didn't get my abilities from a Cracker Jack box," she said, laughing, "and neither did you."

"Me? My abilities?"

She laughed again. "You've noticed you've had some pretty strange encounters and happenings, haven't you?" I could feel my heart jump into my throat and my eyes fill up with tears. I wanted to tell her everything that had ever happened to me on the cosmic scale. I plunged into a sobbing recitation of my life. I had kept so quiet about my journey that it was like a tidal wave was washing through me and I could not talk fast enough.

But Karen stopped me midstream. She smiled and put her hand on my knee. "You have a mission, kid. You're going on eighteen, and it's time you learned about your abilities and how to use them."

Oh God, I thought. "What's my mission?"

She got up and smiled. "Don't worry, you'll find out soon enough. I want you back out here next Friday night. I'm starting my Metaphysics 101 class, and you're in it. Bring your mom too; heaven knows she could use a lot of metaphysics." We walked out. She hugged me and went over to chat with her other guests. Not surprisingly, my mom was over by herself, looking at a book about UFOs and the Bible. She looked so relieved when I walked up, like someone being saved from a shipwreck.

"What's up? What did she say?" Mom asked. On the ride home, I told her of the meeting and how we had been invited to the Metaphysics 101 classes that next Friday night. Mom said, "I'd better come with you and see what this is all about. Are you sure we're not getting into something too far-out?" At this point, I didn't care; I knew I had to do this and it would be the initiation for my mission, whatever that was going to be.

For the next few weeks, I attended Metaphysics 101 and learned about ESP, the paranormal, and the journey of the soul. It was so amazing! I didn't feel like I was learning new things, just expanding and tuning up what I already had within me. But when the last class was over, I was feeling a bit let down. I still wanted more. I had felt like some inner channels had opened, but there was something else stirring within me, something that still wanted to be noticed. I focused on practicing for the singing contest that was now just weeks away and continued going to Karen's center for the Metaphysical Christian services.

One night after the services, Karen approached me. "Hey, kiddo, what are your days off from work?" I told her I had Sundays and Mondays off. She had a little twinkle in her eye like she knew something I didn't. "I want you to come out here on Monday morning at ten, okay?"

"Sure, but why?" I asked.

"All will be revealed in due time," she said with a laugh.

Oh Jesus, I thought. What was up? It seemed like forever before Monday morning came. I arrived fifteen minutes early, and Karen pulled up right when I did. "Ah," she said. "I like a baby psychic that's early. Come on in." I sat down in the waiting area of the center. Karen pulled out a cigarette and plopped herself down on the stool next to the counter. She took a big drag of her cigarette and exhaled, saying, "Kid, today's the day for your trial run."

"My trial run? For what?"

"It's time you started doing psychic readings," she said. "I've told Franny to book you a few today. You know, just to get your feet wet."

"Holy crap!" I said aloud. "I'm not a reader, I'm just a seeker. I can't read anyone, and I'm just, just a kid! And a singer!" I was now standing up with both hands over my mouth in shock.

Again, Karen laughed and said, "How will you know you're not a reader until you try? I trust you. You have a gift, and it's time you used it. I've taught you the basics, and now it's your turn to see what you can do. Oh, by the way, your first client is in ten minutes." She got up, kissed me on the cheek, and walked into her office and closed the door.

Now I was in panic mode. "How the hell am I going to do this?" I said aloud, not knowing that Franny, the other resident psychic, overheard me as she walked into the waiting room.

"You'll do it by the guidance you've been given, sweetie! That's how we all do it." I saw this short, skinny lady walk up to me with open arms. "Welcome, Darrin," she said and gave me a big hug. She walked over to the counter, sat on the same stool where Karen had sat, pulled out a cigarette, and opened a can of Coke. *Gee*, I thought, *what is it with psychics and smoking? Must be an Arkansas psychic thing.*

Franny had a light in her eyes that told me we were going to be very close. She was older than Karen and a past-life reader. She opened the appointment book and said that my first client would be here in a few minutes and that his name was Frank. I guess Franny saw my look of sheer panic; she said, "Don't worry, honey. Spirit won't let you down."

Right then, Frank came through the door. I felt faint. Franny greeted him and said, "Darrin will help you out today. Come this way; I'll show you to his office." *My office*, I thought, *I have an office?* I felt like I was going to pass out on the spot. Suddenly, I heard a voice in my head saying, "She's right — I won't let you down. Go ahead; you'll know what to do." I looked around, and not a soul was in sight that I could see. Well, what else was there to do but do it? Franny came back and said, "Your office is the first door on the left, right next to mine." She took my hand and squeezed it. "Go in."

I walked down the hallway feeling like I was walking the green mile and entered my office. Frank was seated on a couch, and there was my own green velvet reading chair. I sat down, and I could feel a calming energy fall over me. Somehow my desperation was gone.

Frank was tall and really looked out of place. I knew he had never done this before. Little did he know I hadn't either! He seemed weathered by a rough life, like he had been run over by a herd of cattle. "Well," I said, "I bet you're wondering what a kid like me is doing giving psychic readings?"

He laughed. "Well, yes...I thought most psychics were older. Are you any good?"

I laughed nervously. "I don't know. Let's find out, shall we?" He smiled with an odd look on his face, opened his wallet, and took out a photo of a young man. He started crying. I took the picture and placed my hand on it. Frank hadn't said a word about the young man other than acknowledging that this was his son, Tobey. The minute I put my hand on the picture, I surrendered to what was coming to me. Images began to appear in my mind. I realized that Tobey had recently died of AIDS. In psychic midstream, I thought to myself, *Why couldn't I get an easy one, like someone asking if he'll be rich?*

Suddenly the energy shifted in the room. I looked up, and there was Frank's son, an iridescent figure behind Frank's right shoulder. *Oh boy*, I thought, *here we go.* "Frank," I said, "Tobey is here."

Even Frank had felt the shift in the room. "Can you smell his cologne?" Frank asked. He began crying even more. It was a nice confirmation. For the next hour and a half I helped Frank and his son heal a long and rough relationship. Frank had been devastated by Tobey's death and felt it was somehow his fault. To make matters worse, Frank and Tobey were estranged, the result of an argument because Tobey was gay. Tobey died without his father by his side. Frank was afraid AIDS had been a punishment from God and Tobey was in hell.

Deep in Frank's heart, he knew this was not true. He really wanted to tell Tobey he loved him and missed him and that he was sorry. Tobey replied through me that the other side was an awesome place and there was no damnation or hellfire. He was learning so many wonderful things about life and the universe. He went on to tell his dad not to worry; he was filled with love, and all his physical and emotional pain was gone. After the reading, Frank left with a sense of completeness, not only for his son, but also for himself.

When I came out of the office, Franny and Karen were both seated at the counter. "Well," Karen asked, "how did it go?"

Franny answered before I could. "It went great, of course. Look at him, he's shining."

Shining? I thought. *No, I'm trembling.* "I'll be back." I grabbed a cup of coffee and went out the back door. In the backyard, Karen had put in a pond and a little bridge, completely surrounded by trees, a peaceful place to sit and think. I sat on the bridge and watched the goldfish swim below. A cool breeze blew across my face. My thoughts were spinning in my head. Was it my mission to be a psychic? I wasn't sure if I wanted that kind of responsibility. I was only a seventeen-year-old kid, for God's sake. I was dreaming of becoming a singer and entertainer. Now I really had a problem. Visions of distressed people popped in my head, asking for the answers to all their problems and wanting to talk to dead relatives. Was I meant for that? I started feeling sick. It was overwhelming. I was freaked. And what about my singing career?! My mind jumped from one freaky thought to the next. Maybe I could be the singing psychic! It would be a lot like the singing nun, except I would have a sex life, hopefully, and go without the habit. Finally, I took a breath and tried to relax my mind. I wanted to get in touch with that part of myself that could tell me what the hell was going on.

I felt vibrations all around me. I could hear the wind blowing through the trees and the birds singing. About thirty minutes had passed when Franny's shout made me jump. "Darrin, your next client is here."

"Oh, my God," I said aloud. I couldn't believe this was happening. I got up, walked in, and saw my client.

Barbara was seated on the couch. As I sat down, I thought to myself, *Maybe this one just wants to find love.* But even then I knew my readings would never be that vague and shallow. I could feel the same calming energy falling over me again. Barbara opened her purse and took out some photos of her son. She started crying. I took the pictures and placed my hand on them. Again, images began to appear in my mind. She was a single mom, completely at a loss as to how to deal with her son's depression and mood swings. I saw that his father had been abusive and had left them both when her son was twelve; he was now fourteen and still feeling the pain of loss and betrayal. I also saw he was not associating with friends who had his best interests in mind.

The images faded, and in my head I heard a voice say, "Okay, here is the formula of resolution...." I repeated aloud what the voice said. The gist of it was that mother and son needed family counseling so they could learn to talk to each other. The bridge of relationship needed to be rebuilt between them. The son loved his mother very much, but because of their lack of communication, they had drifted apart. She needed to face him with love, and they both had to come together and help heal each other, for she was in just as much pain as he was. Plus, the friends the son was hanging out with were going to be arrested in a few weeks on a burglary charge. Her son would have nothing to do with it, but it would be a wrong-place-at-the-wrong-time kind of deal, and they would try to pin it on him. He needed to clear out from them now.

When I came out of what felt like a trance, Barbara was looking at me with her eyes wide open. "How did you know all that?" she asked.

"Call it intuition," I said. "The main focus here is for you to talk to your son — that's the key. Don't be afraid to talk to him; he needs you right now."

She began to cry again. "You're right. I have shut him out,

just like his father did. I was afraid; I didn't want to talk to him about the divorce, and I just went headlong into my work. He was in so much pain before I realized it. But you're right — I'll have to talk to him." Barbara had come to me as a last-ditch effort to resolve this issue. Sometimes when you are lost in the mists, it's good to have someone shine a light for you. She couldn't afford therapy, so I put her in touch with a counselor friend I knew would be willing to help her. As I walked Barbara to the door, I told her to talk to her son that evening; it would not only help them both, but chances are it would also help to derail any false accusations from his so-called friends. (Later, I would find out, she did talk to him that night, and the healing began for both of them. The son ended his unhealthy relationships. Two weeks after the day of the reading, his ex-friends were arrested.)

I had successfully given my second reading of the day. As I walked out the door, Karen said, "We'll see you next Monday — you're on the team now, kid!" I got in my car and drove home. I was still in a state of shock and too stunned to talk about my feelings. It was hard for me to believe that I had become a channel of spiritual direction, and so soon. I still felt wet behind the ears. I had thought it took years to learn about this stuff. And on top of everything else, to be a counselor-type psychic — not just a fortune-teller — right from the get-go. It was a lot for a seventeen-year-old to take on. But it seemed I had no choice.

While driving that evening, I struggled with the dilemma I faced. *You've put me in an interesting situation*, I told the Gods. *Do you realize that I have a singing contest in a week? I could become the next Judy Garland...only a male version...and without the drug habit!* But I knew in my heart what I had to do. Singing was my passion, but being a psychic guide was my mission. I knew it. But I was not going to let the Gods get away with it that easy. I went on to demand, *I want a sign from you. If my mission is to be a psychic guide, then I want a big fat s—*. Before I could finish the sentence, a green and gold shooting star streaked across the night sky, right in front of me. I slammed on the brakes and stopped the car. I got out and stood in the middle of the highway, looking up at the sky. I kept saying aloud, "Oh my God, Oh my God!" Then a voice in my head said, "You happy now?" I felt like I was in an *X-Files* episode. Freaked out, I jumped in the car and sped home. Destiny had spoken.

That day was the beginning of my career as a psychic. I began giving regular readings. Eventually I opened an office, where I offered psychic advice and taught workshops on metaphysics and spiritual growth. I loved every minute of it. I didn't give up my singing. I incorporated my musical passions into my work as much as possible.

Getting Ready to Take My Teaching to a New Level

About the time I turned twenty-six, I started feeling burned out. I had placed a heavy responsibility on my own shoulders and felt like I had to help every person who crossed my path. I was frequently doing eight readings a day, each lasting anywhere from an hour to an hour and a half. Most weekends, I was teaching seminars and workshops. People called and demanded readings and psychic advice all the time. The stress was too much. While helping everyone else find themselves, I was losing myself.

I started learning about boundaries and how to say no. But

another stress factor arose: I started drawing groupies and even a few stalkers. Somehow I was becoming like a guru. It was no fun at all. I felt I needed to be perfect so I could help people 100 percent. I was my own worst critic, always berating myself when I thought I fell short of what I was supposed to be, especially if I didn't practice what I preached. Carrying all of this was a very heavy load, and I felt I needed a break to reevaluate my life, and myself. I had somehow lost the passion of my mission and forgot that the inspiration had come from the divine.

I pulled up the reigns and brought everything to a halt. I got rid of the so-called friends who could not live without their twenty-four-hour on-call psychic advisor, and I canceled future readings and seminars. Darrin Owens, psychic, was on leave. For the first time in years, I took time off for myself. I wanted to get back in sync with my mystical self and regain the passion that I knew I had lost. I left Arkansas and moved to Indianapolis, where I went to work for a production company that specialized in creating workshops for some of the leading teachers in the spiritual field.

My new job allowed me access to some wonderful teachers, and for the first time in a long time I got to wear the student hat again. Each teacher had his or her own twist on spiritual teaching. Some of their approaches inspired me, and some gave me pause. As I worked behind the scenes, I came to realize that everyone is human and has his or her own karma to deal with. I realize now that after years of helping others grow up, it was simply my turn. These experiences made me want to walk my talk, or at least try my best to do so. I had learned long before that we are meant to have teachers in our lives, but they are not meant to replace the teacher within ourselves.

During my three-year hiatus, I tried my hand at different things — all of which would prove to be useful later. I worked as a publicist/agent and meeting planner and learned a lot about the marketing field and media. I had great fun booking actors, authors, and entertainers for magazine or radio spots and setting up seminars. I even thought about starting my singing career again. I have to say I enjoyed not having to deal with anyone else's emotional issues, not getting phone calls about house hauntings, and not teaching. I had my own inner crap to deal with. But I felt something stirring again in my gut. It was the same stirring that pulled me to go deeper into myself, a cosmic push.

After turning twenty-eight, the day came when my vacation was over. It was time to begin my mission once more as a spiritual guide and teacher. It was time for a comeback! The message to return didn't come through anything exciting like a car wreck or a near-fatal sickness; it was a quiet nudge one night while I was watching TV. You know how your brain just goes numb sometimes while watching the tube? Well that's when the Gods snuck in. The voice in my head told me, "Darrin, it's time to begin again. You have a mission, and it's time to go." That was it, plain and simple. I have learned that when the Gods say go, you go.

I can't believe I'm going back to Little Rock. This thought repeated itself in my head the entire drive home. When I had left for Indianapolis over three years earlier, I had decided I would never go back. As I drove past the WELCOME TO ARKANSAS sign, I remembered the saying, "If you want to make God laugh, make a plan." In response to my planning never to come back, God had eventually landed me here, on the interstate, en route to just the place I had vowed to stay away from. And now I felt a welcoming sense of homecoming, of balance, and of destiny. I felt comfortable, having learned that the universe knows better than we do about life's journeys and destinations.

I drove into the Little Rock city limits and pulled into the Barnes & Noble parking lot. It was February, a mild month in Arkansas, but there was still a chill in the air. I wrapped my arms around myself and walked into the bookstore to meet my friend Carol. She had been my manager when I worked as a bookseller there six years earlier.

Through the years Carol had become one of my closest friends and biggest fans. Our meeting, years before, had been a catalyst for Carol's spiritual journey. Now, along with being my business manager, she has become an advanced astrologer and a pretty good intuitive in her own right. Who knew a woman married to a Baptist minister would become a New Age junkie! The Lord works in mysterious ways.

I walked through the front entrance of the store, and before I knew what was happening, a pair of lips came out of nowhere and found my cheek. "Oh my God, you made it. You're here. I cannot believe this!" I didn't know how Carol could talk and kiss at the same time, but she always bragged about being a master at multitasking.

After this dramatic greeting, which drew stares from several curious customers, Carol and I sat down for coffee. I allowed myself to take a deep breath, and the steam from the latte filled my nostrils. For some reason, it felt like I had been holding my breath the entire trip back, and now I could relax.

I was in Little Rock to resume my work as a psychic and teacher — and now, for the first time, as a writer. Coming

home seemed to have brought me full circle. After a long journey, I was returning home to another level of myself. In the
months that followed, I began writing down the spiritual wisdom I had gleaned during my years as a psychic and psychic-
in-hiding. The chapters that follow are a result of that work.

CHAPTER TWO

THE SEVENFOLD PATH
OF SPIRITUAL GROWTH

$\mathcal{B}$eginning in ancient times and continuing for many thousands of years, people drawn to the spiritual path were led to holy temples, esoteric orders, and mystery schools. In these places, masters prepared seekers for journeys deep within themselves. By teaching them the secrets of claiming inner power and controlling their inner dynamics, the masters initiated seekers into the life of the mystic. This began the life-long process of achieving higher states of consciousness through experiencing the divine.

The ancient mystery schools are a thing of the past — but no matter. You can make your life a mystery school if you approach it in the right way. Every time you meet someone, every time you encounter a challenging situation, the divine teacher is asking you to free yourself from the mortal mind and to embrace the mystical. The mystical world is always there, offering you its power.

Even though everyday life is the only mystery school you need, an initiation is still important. Without the power and commitment of initiation, our eyes remain set on the fixed destination and not the journey itself, and we miss the opportunities life provides for us; we forget too easily the importance of stepping into spirit with ease and pure intent.

What I offer in the rest of this book is a curriculum for initiation into the mystery school of life. One by one, each chapter will guide you toward greater awareness of your own divine nature and how to tap into it to gain greater satisfaction in life. If you listen with your soul and put the ideas into practice, you will develop your intuition and become more sensitive to the mystical world. Once you've explored all seven topics, you'll be ready to continue your journey on your own. You'll have graduated from Darrin Owens's modern mystery school.

Mapping the Path

Over many years of working with clients and students (and myself!), I've seen a common pattern of spiritual development. Many people go through particular stages in a certain order. Learning the lessons of one stage is what prepares them to enter the next stage. Once they download one piece of divine inspiration, they are ready for the next. The common pattern is to pass through seven different stages, which can be called Spiritual Awakening, Divine Darkness, Interior Power, Inner Attunement, Conscious Creation, Wholistic Living, and Oneness.

But that's putting it too simply. The stages manifest differently for each person. Not everyone goes through them in the same order. And more important, once you pass through one "stage" and into another, you aren't necessarily done with the earlier one. You can be well into the sixth stage but then have to deal with issues you thought you had mastered in the fourth stage. In other words, the stages can overlap, be simultaneous, or crop up more than once.

So it isn't quite right to call the seven stages *stages*. They don't work that way for people, and they don't form a straight line to the goal of enlightenment. In a way, this should be obvious: the Gods aren't logical, and they don't follow a prewritten script. That's how they keep us on our toes.

Instead of seven stages, we are dealing with something closer to seven essential components, or elements, of spiritual growth. The seven elements appear here in linear order because they have to be that way in a book. This might be a little too logical for the Gods, but it should help you track your growth more easily.

Approaching the Seven Elements

I suggest that you ponder and work with each element as it appears in this book. You may already be familiar with the experiences and issues of some elements. In fact, it is likely that you've already experienced — or are in the process of experiencing — the first element, spiritual awakening, because your awakening process is what prompted you to pick up this book in the first place.

Remember that spiritual growth is an evolutionary journey. Don't think about how long it will take you to master an element, to transform it from knowledge to wisdom — just allow your intuition to guide you through it at your own pace.

Go with what feels safe and comfortable to you. Above all, re-member that the truths you seek are within you and nowhere else. No one else has the same connection to or perception of the divine that you have. In other words, don't get freaked if you find yourself dealing with element five when you haven't yet had the experiences of element four; you will find all of them inside you in due time.

The lessons contained within each of the seven elements are powerful catalysts for change. They are designed to open the spiritual centers within you, to release the potentials of your spiritual energy. This can be a scary process. Your heart can recognize a spiritual truth and tell you, "Yes! For God's sake, listen!" But then your mortal mind, working from fear, can jump in and say, "Well, I don't know; I'll have to figure this out." That's the point when you can lose the inspiration and begin to pick apart the wisdom until there's nothing left. You can end up saying it didn't work, but the truth is you never let it work for you in the first place. The only way out of fear-based thinking is to face the fear, understand the reasons why it takes over, and change those dynamics.

It's also important to remember that spiritual teachings are not difficult to embody. If they were, the Gods would have nothing to do with them. The emotional task of living a les-son may be difficult, but ultimately the wisdom that comes from it is easy to incorporate into your soul. We tend to make spirituality so detailed and full of rights and wrongs that we run the risk of leaving spirit out of it. Our mortal minds want to rationalize everything and figure it out, but the divine is meant to be experienced, not figured out. Remember this while you explore the seven elements — they are written to help you stay as simple as possible with your spirituality.

Invoking the Sacred and Living the Lessons

At the end of each chapter, there is a mystical invocation, or prayer. These are alchemical formulas, meant to be read aloud or spoken with sacred intent in your mind. They will help to invoke the sacred presence in everyday life, to guide you into a deeper relationship with the divine.

Each prayer is formulated to enhance the divine power of the lessons in the chapter. In prayer we commune with and connect to a higher source through a focused intention. Feel free to change each prayer to suit your own vision of the divine, so that you remain open to experiencing each particular mystical power. For example, where the prayer has *divine presence*, you may want to say *God* or *Divine Mother* instead.

I suggest repeating each invocation or prayer three times. Three is always a good activation number, and it helps the mind know that you mean business. Plus, it tells the Gods that your intent is truly to change your mind and lifestyle.

I have also added what I call Wisdom Tips after each chapter. The Wisdom Tips are practical guidelines to help you exemplify each stage of soul development with more ease and understanding.

Continuing Your Growth

If you think of yourself as a student in the mystery school of life, you will recognize — as an ancient mystic would — that the spiritual journey is a lifelong process. This approach is a necessary antidote to today's quick-fix attitude. We want enlightenment now without the dirt work. When enlightenment doesn't happen, we get bored and find ourselves hopping from one guru or belief to another.

The seven elements contain lifelong lessons that you will always be running into. Spiritual growth is not a contest; you don't win and then go on a free vacation on cloud nine for the rest of your life. You become more and more conscious on many different levels throughout your life. Successfully ending an unhealthy addiction or getting through a personal crisis doesn't mean your growth is over. You will go on to download another facet of spiritual power. The universe is a vast array of spiritual wisdom that is hidden in every cosmic molecule of life.

When I teach my Mystics Mystery School, it lasts several days and is very intense, but I tell all my students that the real lessons happen after they leave the classroom. Life is the true test of each lesson, where the learning really happens. The same is true of this book: just reading the chapters is not enough.

Being a Light for the World

The purpose of spiritual growth is not just to heal your soul and change your life for the better; it's also to benefit those around you. The Gods train us to see clearly in order to help those around us to do the same. When one enlightened person sees the light, others will too. This doesn't mean you should go off to some street corner and start preaching the gospel — that's not how the Gods like the light to be spread around. All you have to do is be you. Others will see that something in you has changed, and they will begin to feel a difference within themselves and begin to seek their own path. You may be the light post or the guidepost; it doesn't matter which.

Think about Christ. It has been told that all he did was walk around and spread his gospel. But that isn't the whole story. He had an inner light that was seen by every person that came into contact with him. He did not have to shout from the rooftops, "I'm a child of God! Hear me!" People knew that his inner light was divine. In this way he could work as a sacred catalyst, transforming the world by opening hearts.

Some people are open to divinely inspired personal change, and some are not. The question is, are you someone who is open? If so, you know that authentic, heart-centered practice will change your life. When you connect with the divine at a deeper level, there is nothing to do but change for the better.

CHAPTER THREE

Spiritual Awakening

Spiritual Awakening is the beginning of the journey of self-discovery. It happens when you begin to see a sliver of the divine in your life. It's as if your spiritual eyes begin to open from a deep sleep, just enough to see the new morning light. When the awakening process is complete, and your spiritual eyes are fully open, you are conscious of your divine nature and you know that there is a divine purpose in everything.

Becoming aware of the divine force in your life is really just a matter of remembering. Somehow in life, we forget the line in life's script that says we are part of a divine reality. Because spirit is our essence, we have always been on the path of spirit; each person just has to remember and reenergize that truth. It's like discovering a secret code and then breaking that code bit by bit.

During your awakening you have an incredible cast of angels and guides for spiritual support. They just wait for the day that you begin to wander outside of your familiar mental box. Then this scramble of spirits prepares the path for you and sets up situations for your learning. Remember: the universe itself is always pushing you toward realizing your higher potential.

Calling the Cosmic 911 Line

The power of Awakening must be called into your life. Whether or not you believe in God or another form of divine being, you open the door to the universe of unlimited wisdom and potential when you ask the questions, "Who am I?" "Why am I here?" and "Is this all there is?" The magical power of asking why sets the stage for your spiritual journey, revealing a mysterious and vast dimension that was always there. Your desire to know more, to expand awareness from the physical to the mystical, is what invokes the presence of the Gods.

In *The Wizard of Oz*, Dorothy longs for a deeper meaning in life. If others can travel beyond the world she can see, she asks, "Why, oh why, can't I?" The result is a dramatic awakening: she gets a cyclone trip to a brand-new world. A yellow-brick road is laid before her that she must follow in order to fulfill her destiny and gain further spiritual awareness. This is basically what we all go through during the Awakening stage.

How does a person get into the kind of mind frame that lands him or her at the door of Awakening? What directs someone to question her or his existence? Awakenings often happen through crises. You can be going through life thinking you are on the mark and nothing can stop you, and then *boom*, you trip over a rock in the path. You find out your partner has left or you lose your job. You cry to yourself, "Where did that come from? I thought I had everything under control." Or you may be struggling through life, fearful of every turn in the road, when you hit rock bottom. Knowing that something has to change, you call out to the heavens, "Where did I go wrong?" You call the cosmic 911 line.

In my early life, I often wondered if I had any hope for a happy life. During that time, I realized there was something urging me to keep going. I am not sure how the subtle message of hope got through my teen angst. But thank God it did, and after hitting rock bottom, I had nothing left to do but listen. The divine presence is confident that we will eventually give up control and let ourselves be guided. The divine force nudges us into the unknown territory within ourselves. And moments of crisis can send us on a one-way, all-expenses-paid trip to wake-up time.

Awakenings can happen through blessings as well. I have talked to people who witnessed a birth, visited a sacred site, or just read a line in a book, and then everything changed. In an instant, something rewired their thoughts. A friend of mine offers a good example. When we were having coffee one day, I mentioned a book I thought she should read. She was dealing with some personal issues, and the book I was recommending had really helped me through similar circumstances. She agreed to read it, but I knew it was not at the top of her list. Since she was a fast-track career woman with an "I want it now" edge, reading a book and doing inner work was not something she looked forward to. The next week she flew to London for a business meeting. As soon as she walked into the lobby of her hotel, she saw the book I had told her about, lying on a table in front of her. Someone had left it there. She ignored it as chance at first. But she was faced with this book every morning when she walked through the lobby to her meetings. Finally, she gave in and took the book to her room and read all night. Ever since that experience she has had a change of heart and mind. She took the cosmic hint, accepting the guidance offered her. The synchronicity of the book appearing in her life of its own accord opened her eyes to something that was revealing itself to her.

In an instant, a simple act of divine intervention can redirect you, guiding you onto a more spiritual path. But whatever route you take — crisis or blessing — the road always leads back to you, and that is always a blessing. How readily you open your mind to the divine presence is up to you. Depending on how hardheaded you are, the Gods may use either a gentle push or a sledgehammer to get your attention. For most people, myself included, it takes a few kicks in the astral before you really begin to wake up. But all that matters is that the Awakening eventually happens. The power of Awakening pushes you inward to find a deeper, more authentic part of yourself.

The Sacred Catalyst

A power, an intelligent energy, swirls around those who are experiencing Awakening. I've experienced it psychically in countless readings and seminars, and in my own life. I call this energy the *sacred catalyst*. The sacred catalyst is an aspect of divine energy and is sent by the Gods to be your spiritual engineer. Its job is to rewire you, to prepare you for shifting from a physical life to a mystical life.

The sacred catalyst actually makes its appearance long before Awakening is manifest. It sets you up in a life situation designed to make you seek a deeper purpose. As I explained earlier, this life situation leads either to a crashing-down crisis or an uplifting revelatory blessing. This is the sacred catalyst's main job — to create a catalytic event that makes you wake up and take notice of your soul and its spiritual destiny.

The sacred catalyst is not out to harm or punish anyone, even though a person under its influence may feel that way at first. It's just that a little divine chaos is necessary for making change. Spiritual Awakening is a profound realization — how can a person experience that truth without his or her physical world going a little topsy-turvy? How can you change your mind from the negative to the positive if you never have anything to rock the boat you're sailing in?

With its shaking-up power, the sacred catalyst awakens the truth that you are not in control and that there is a higher power running the show. Far from removing from you the responsibility for your own destiny, this realization gives responsibility back to you. You understand that it's your choice to follow divine guidance or not. This is the beginning of spiritual self-reliance. You know you are the owner of your thoughts and you can no longer play the blame game or the victim game. You have awakened and now have the power of spiritual insight to guide you farther down your yellow-brick road. With this insight, you become ever more conscious, clearing everything that is keeping heaven's light from shining within you.

There is no going back once the Awakening stage is activated and the sacred catalyst's energy is downloaded into your system, directing you toward your destiny. This doesn't mean there won't be more bumps in the road. But after your Spiritual Awakening, the bumps won't be roadblocks anymore. You'll be able to maneuver around them with your newfound insight and spiritual self-reliance. And just in case you get too caught up in negative thinking or neglect your mystical mind, the sacred catalyst — in all its swirling chaotic glory — will always be there to shake things up and keep you awake.

Sometimes particular people can themselves embody the sacred catalyst energy or archetype. In general, the people who channel this energy are those who activate change, who make a wave or a splash in life. On the grand scale, such people as Gloria Steinem, Martin Luther King Jr., and the Dalai Lama are good examples of channels for the sacred catalyst; they created catalytic events that brought a positive change to the global mind. But on the small scale, I think this divine chaotic power uses me as its channel from time to time. There have been moments when I've walked into a room and all heaven has broken loose. What I mean is that people's "stuff" tends to be activated if they are around me for a certain length of time. But being a spiritual teacher, I don't think this is that unusual. Each of us can be a sacred catalyst for positive change. Whether we want to believe it or not, change in any form has a divine purpose and is leading us in a positive direction.

Avoiding Psychic Glamour

When you enter the Awakening process, there is a danger of getting stuck in what I call the psychic glamour factory. Let me explain with an example. In *Charlie and the Chocolate Factory*, the candy maker Willy Wonka allows the children to enter his wondrous factory, and they go crazy, wanting to taste everything in sight. Well, you may feel like this at the beginning of your Awakening. You are tempted to read everything spiritual or metaphysical you can get your hands on, go to every self-help workshop, visit one psychic or healer after another, and so on. When you first start to open your eyes to spirit and taste a bit of that divine flavor, you are truly like a kid in a candy factory.

But you have to be careful not to get stuck in the candy factory and become addicted to the glamorous sweetness of the spiritual journey. It may be sweet and taste good, but after a while you will overdose on it and the sweetness turns to poison. You can get stuck in the illusionary, ego-based thought mode that says the spiritual journey is about attaining spiritual or psychic talents. This is one reason why I don't teach people to be psychics — in my opinion, it would lead too many people into glamour. The idea of labeling oneself a healer or psychic is just too attractive to many people.

Succumbing to the false allure of the spiritual glamour factory distracts you from your true connection to the divine. You can get attracted like a moth to a flame to all the light and action of flashy psychic phenomena, such as ESP, spontaneous healings, apparitions, aura readings, talking to the dead, talking to angels and spirit guides, and so on — the kind of stuff a two-bit fortune-teller would market at a psychic fair. Yes, these phenomena are real powers of spirit, but seeking them should not be what guides you on the spiritual path. They may come to you naturally, as by-products of spiritual growth, if they're meant to; don't try to force it.

The ability to communicate directly with spiritual entities is a privilege granted to some of us. Being a healer or psychic is something that is ordained; if the Gods have given you this calling, you'll know it. If you find yourself becoming more intuitive or find that the power of healing comes easy for you, great. The Gods will lead you farther on this path. You do not have to direct your calling.

Some time ago, I was reunited with friends I hadn't seen for two or three years. Their Awakening process had been sidetracked by glamour, and to my surprise that's where they remained. They told me of a new how-to psychic course they were in and the other classes they had been flip-flopping around in. It was just like what they had been doing years before. They had kept running around in psychic circles and never once took notice of their inner selves, where the real work was waiting for them. All they could talk about was the new psychic tricks they could perform — or thought they could perform.

The best way to avoid the trap of the psychic glamour factory is to keep close tabs on your intent. Your intention should be to grow more with the divine, not to develop psychic powers. Don't make Spiritual Awakening a self-esteem issue, something you do to gain egotistical power. Awakening is not about the Gods handing you an application for a cool New Age position.

Once I was doing a reading on a massage therapist who was desperate to become a *healer*. To put it in more positive terms, she was in love with the label of healer. A healer was exactly what she was — but because she was caught up in the glamour of what she thought a healer was supposed to be, she missed that fact totally. She told me that she wanted people to touch the hem of her garment and be healed. At that point, I knew that despite her abilities she could never become a true healer unless she dropped the messiah complex and realized the healing had to begin within herself.

The Journey Ahead

When you experience Awakening, you behold a new world. Then you begin a journey to chart more territories of that world within you. The sacred core of Awakening is that you start becoming more aware that you are part of something larger than yourself. You have asked the magic question — "Why?" — and now your mission is to understand the mystery that is life and to move toward experiencing oneness with the divine.

Spiritual Awakening brings to you the perception that you can see and experience the divine in everything, even within yourself. It's one of the hardest things to comprehend — that each of us is essentially part of the divine. For so many years, especially here in the West, God has been said to be outside of us and separate. This is far from the truth. God is not something out there, but something living in each of us. This is the truth that must become part of your consciousness before you take up the other six elements of spiritual growth.

Awakening is purely a preparation for true spiritual growth. When Awakening happens, it prepares you for descent into a deeper territory. Spirit is within the depths of your being, and there is only one way to go — down. It's like a staircase to a dark cellar. The reason it's dark is because we have to face our fears there. The Awakening lesson opens the door to our inner cellar, and we begin to step down into it. It sounds paradoxical, but the deeper you go within yourself, the higher your consciousness is raised.

Spiritual Awakening Prayer

Divine Spirit, I awaken to your very presence within my being. I open my heart, my mind, my soul to your holy light. May your sacred vibration of wisdom infuse my mind with knowledge and banish all fear. I realize the truth that I am not alone and I am your child.

May your very breath of life enter my body and awaken the sleeping corners of my soul. I awaken to your truth. I awaken to your wisdom. I awaken to your Holy Spirit. Come, Holy Spirit, and wash the sleep from my eyes so that I may now see the newness of your gifts and creation. I am awake, I am alive, and I am ready to live the mystical life. I accept this blessing here and now.

Divine Spirit, I thank you.

Wisdom Tips for Spiritual Awakening

1. Begin reading spiritual literature and attending seminars on spiritual growth and self improvement — and I don't mean books or classes that promise you psychic powers in sixty seconds! You know how I feel about that. Have fun and explore this new mystical world.

2. Listen to upbeat new age, classical, or international music. This helps the spiritual centers within you open up and take charge.

3. Talk with friends you can trust about your Awak-
    enings and start a group of support that you can
    meet with regularly.

4. Remember to be open to change. When your
    Awakening is manifesting, the sacred catalyst is
    directing you to a higher perspective.

CHAPTER FOUR

DIVINE DARKNESS

Spiritual Awakening begins the process of soul development and reveals that you are part of divinity. But in doing
that, it sheds light on what needs to change in your life. Divine
Darkness, the next stage, is usually not far behind. It asks you
to embrace and make those changes, to confront the false
inner voices and beliefs that direct your life in order to release
yourself from their limitations. During the phase of Divine
Darkness, you move through the veils of illusion to a place of
authentic realization.

Divine Darkness is a bittersweet stage for the soul. But essentially, Spiritual Awakening and Divine Darkness work together, hand in hand, to make room for the other five elements
to come into your life. You can think of Awakening as the ar-
rival of the sunlight that the seedling of spirit needs in order
to sprout, and Divine Darkness as the deep, cool earth that

gives the seedling the nutrients and life force it needs to continue growing. To use another metaphor, if Awakening is when you open your spiritual eyes, then Divine Darkness is when you wipe the sleep from them. It's when you begin to slough off those crusty, irritating habits, illusions, and thoughts that glued your spiritual eyelids shut.

During Awakening, you prayed to the Gods, asking to know more, to feel more, and to experience more. The only way to have this prayer answered is to meet the divine in the darkness of your own soul, where all the fears and false inner voices lie. Your task is to face those fears, to quiet those inner voices — to strip away all the distractions that have prevented the light of the divine from shining through.

In Divine Darkness, you are challenged to live in alone time. You come face to face with you, in the presence of the divine. It's a scary process. It may feel as if life as you once knew it is over, as if you are floating in a sort of cosmic limbo. You may experience what some mystics and saints have called the "dark night of the soul."

Divine Darkness is not all about looking at the bad though; in the end it's really about reclaiming the good and coming into full possession of your strengths. Experiencing this part of your growth will stretch you to your limits — but it is what allows you to become limitless. You dive deep into the unknown to find what is known. You go through the darkness to see the light.

The Purification of the Soul

After Spiritual Awakening comes the task of inner cleansing, or purifying the soul. This means stripping away what is not real and not true. It means revealing your false self for what it is and refusing to listen to what that false self has always told you. Letting go of the parts of yourself that you have believed in for so long is not an easy thing to do. That is why the journey of the soul is not always bright lights and angels' voices. It can be like wrestling with the devil in a desert. The challenge of waking up and seeing what is real also means seeing what is not real.

It is the fear-based self that keeps you from growing. It says that if you change, you will get hurt, fail, or be laughed at. This is the voice you must detach from and move beyond. When I was dealing with my dark time, it felt like I was lost in the perpetual darkness of a cave. Every turn seemed to lead to another dark passage. As I walked in my own dark night, I witnessed the part of me that was scared to death of the world. It was the part of me that believed the fear that I had been taught. It was the source of the voice that said, "You're stupid" and "You can't do that!" My challenge at that time in my life was to face this part of myself head-on and boot it out of my soul.

Purification of the soul begins to happen during the Awakening stage, but Divine Darkness is what finishes the job. The mystical darkness is that cleansing. It causes a breakdown in your emotional and physical life that disrupts all your old patterns. It helps you separate from people, places, and things that no longer serve your higher good and are not healthy for you. This process often brings on the feeling of living in two different worlds. Part of you remains grounded in the physical world of survival, while another part is awakening to a spiritual life. You are filled with a desire for mystical experiences but overwhelmed with a fear that those experiences will dismantle your secure and comfortable physical world.

As you go through this crisis, you need to remember that the disruption of your emotional and physical life is what leads to a breakthrough in your spiritual life. Purification leads to illumination, the realization of your potential. When you purify your soul, the new can enter only because you have let go of the old.

Divine Guidance

Divine guidance is what leads you out of the darkness and toward illumination. By listening to divine guidance, you learn how to construct an inner pathway in the mind and heart that allows for a spiritual existence in the physical world.

In my seminars people often ask me, "How do I know the voice of divine guidance?" "How do I know when the Gods are speaking to me?" When I hear this kind of question, I know that the person asking it is still going through the purification process and hasn't learned what I call the *power of discernment*. When you've stripped away the distractions within and have learned how to ignore all the voices that come from a place of fear, you can discern the voice of the divine. The false, fear-based voices were implanted in your mind by experience, but the voice of the divine — simple, direct, and loving — has always been within you. It says, "You can do it — keep going" or, "You know better than to think that!" It can be as simple as a calming feeling that comes out of nowhere.

Fear is something you were taught, and love is something you were born with. When you've learned to discern the voice of fear from the voice of love, the voice of fear begins to drift away. You no longer pay attention to it, and fear cannot exist without attention. Conversely, as you begin to pay closer attention to divine guidance it becomes stronger within you.

The divine presence will not whisper winning lotto numbers in your ear or tell you that Mr. Right is just around the corner. The divine will simply guide you, as the word *guidance* implies. It keeps you on your path and tells you when you might be starting to stray off of it. In other words, divine guidance keeps you manifesting the destiny that is all your own. To use a different metaphor, divine guidance keeps you in touch with what author and spiritual teacher Caroline Myss calls your "sacred contract," the destiny that is all your own.[*]

The Heart of Darkness

Divine darkness takes you directly into your heart, to the core of your emotional self. If you are going to hide anything out of fear, you put it in your heart and then repress it. And it's the heart that runs the show. So, the Gods usually make you focus on your heart first. When you get more in touch with emotion — when you listen to your heart — you regain passion for living, for the divine, for your continuing journey into yourself.

To understand the importance of getting to the "heart" of your issues in the Divine Darkness stage, imagine that you are in a beautiful garden at midnight, with only the moon to shed light on your surroundings. Think of the garden as your heart, the moonlight as divine spirit. Some places in the garden are illuminated by the moonlight, and some are not. The

---

[*] Caroline Myss, PhD, *The Anatomy of the Spirit: The Seven Stages of Power and Healing* (New York: Three Rivers, 1996), 67.

places in darkness are the places in your heart where Divine Spirit needs to shine. What keeps those places from sight are your fearful thoughts. Part of you wants those places kept in the dark so you don't have to deal with them. Well, now is the time to deal with them. No matter what your situation, you have chosen to grow up spiritually, and that means anything in your life that keeps you from that growth must be dealt with. In the midst of Divine Darkness, you can choose to dispel the darkness and let the moonlight shine everywhere in the garden of your heart.

When you begin to visit the places that scare you, you will see the light of love there. The dark places carry the keys to unlocking your potential. They hold quiet strength. Through all the fear, pain, and trauma, you can find this strength. You just have to go there. Getting to the heart of your soul will direct you out of the darkness and into the light. You only need to see and remove all the distractions that block the divine light.

The Power of Faith

Divine Darkness asks you to choose which power in your life you will trust: love, the power within, or fear, the power without. The Gods want nothing more than to help you create a life of harmony and ease. In order for that to happen, you have to surrender into love as the power that will direct you. Surrendering to love, to the mystery of it all, means loosening the grip of fear and letting your soul direct your life. It means putting your trust in the heavens and in yourself, refusing to relinquish your power to the outside world or anyone else. This is nothing less than faith.

There is no such thing as having no faith. When someone says to me, "I lost my faith," I reply, "no you didn't; you chose to have faith in something else besides your soul." Faith is not believing in something outside of you; it is knowing where your inner power comes from. It is knowing that you are an energy-being and that you are directed by the energy you choose to live by.

This kind of faith will give you the emotional means to be okay when things aren't so great in your life. When faith comes from the divine, it creates a strong inner stamina that does not react to the illusory reality of the outside world. Divine Darkness teaches you that the reality that matters is on the inside and that the power of faith is a blessing you are entitled to.

Divine Darkness Prayer

Divine presence in the universe, I dive deep into the caves of my soul. With every step, I go deeper into landscapes unknown. I invoke your Holy Spirit to light my way. Reveal to me the hidden treasures that lie before me. These treasures are stepping-stones to enlightened knowledge. With every thought of love, a lamp is lit within my soul. I begin to see and experience you, Holy Spirit. You breathe life into faded memories of love, and hope is renewed. I live in the light. I will not fear the dark, for you are there. You are everywhere, and darkness cannot hide you or me.

Together, Divine Spirit, we walk through the steep and narrow valleys, only to see that the kingdom of the divine awaits my return. Through the darkness the light shall appear. With this prayer I turn on the light, and you, Holy Spirit, are there. I accept this blessing here and now, and I thank you.

Wisdom Tips for Divine Darkness

1. Create alone time. It's essential to have time alone during this period. You need to listen to your inner voice and quiet the mind so the soul can speak.
2. Walk in nature. Mother Earth is a tremendous purifier. The darkness can be confusing at times, so take a walk in the woods or on the beach and clear out the mental clutter.
3. Have a friend or partner you can talk to. You do not need someone to fix your problem, just someone to witness where you are in your growth. Spiritual and emotional support are essential.
4. Pray. Begin a prayerful life and begin to connect with the divine. This is essential and goes with your alone time — it's just you and God in the dark.

CHAPTER FIVE

INTERIOR POWER AND SACRED ENERGY

Once you have cleansed your soul of the illusions that have limited you, you are ready to ascend out of the darkness. Now that you understand the source of divinity, you can move toward the light by learning how to access the energy of the divine. This energy is all around us, vibrating through our bodies and all matter. You simply have to become more aware of it and understand how to use it in your spiritual development. As you do so, you will build Interior Power, the inner strength you need to further your spiritual development.

Divine energy is the universal force that keeps everything in motion and breathes life into all beings. It is recognized in all the world's religious and mystical traditions — as the life force, *prana* (in Sanskrit), *chi* (in Chinese), or the creative energy of God. Our bodies and minds were created to manifest, project, and control this Sacred Energy. The problem is, most of us have forgotten how to be its master.

This chapter is the beginning of your retraining program. Here I cover the basics of how Sacred Energy works and how you can take control of it to build your Interior Power. Interior Power will then become the spiritual stamina you can tap into to transform your life from within.

Spiritual Anatomy and the Chakra System

The divine expresses itself as energy within us. This energy is the soul. Our physical body acts as a temple to this energy, as a place for divine energy to flow and vibrate. It's possible to map how the divine energy moves within the body, how it manifests itself in different ways in different locations. This is our spiritual anatomy, or what author and spiritual teacher Caroline Myss calls our "energy anatomy."*

We humans have been aware of our spiritual anatomy for a very long time. By as early as 2000 BCE, the ancient Hindus had already mapped it out in the form of the *chakra system*. In my opinion, the chakra system is still the best way of understanding spiritual anatomy and the dynamics of the human energy system.

---

* Caroline Myss discusses this concept in her workshops and lectures. For more information, see her book *Anatomy of the Spirit: The Seven Stages of Power and Healing* (New York: Three Rivers, 1996).

A chakra is an energy center in the body. Seven of these energy centers align vertically along the spinal column. *Chakra* means "wheel," so we have seven wheels of spinning energy from the base of the spine (the first chakra) to the top of the head (the seventh chakra). Each chakra corresponds to one of the seven colors of the rainbow and each vibrates to one of the seven notes of the musical scale. I and many other psychics have seen the colors and felt the tones vibrating within the human body. If you have not already witnessed this energy, over time you may be able to develop the skill to perceive it yourself.

Each chakra is associated with a certain part of the body and a certain organ. So when the energy in the chakras is blocked or misdirected, emotional or physical illness can result. Conversely, when the chakras are kept clear, you experience well-being. These seven power centers reflect not only your physical health, but your psychological, emotional, and spiritual states as well.

Each chakra also corresponds to a specific aspect of being. The lower three chakras are associated with physical needs, the fundamental emotions, and the ego. The third chakra, for example, is the center for self-esteem and personal power. The upper four chakras have a connection to our higher emotional and spiritual faculties.

I've summarized the important aspects of the seven chakras in the table that follows. These are very simple descriptions. You can learn much more from other books that focus on the topic. But this table gives you an idea of how important the chakras are to the everyday mystic.

The Chakra System				
Chakra	Location	Color	Life issue	Symptoms of blockage or unbalance
First	Base of spine	Red	Grounding, physical security	Insecurity, fear of the outside world
Second	Sexual organs	Orange	Sexuality, money, creativity, relationships	Guilt, financial worry, sexual frustration
Third	Solar plexus	Yellow	Self-esteem, personal power, courage, honor	Loss of personal power, low self-esteem, sensitivity to criticism
Fourth	Heart/ chest	Green	Love, forgive-ness, emotional health	Anger, hatred
Fifth	Throat	Blue	Surrender, choice, will, self-expression	Judgment of others, addiction
Sixth	Forehead	Indigo	Mystical vision, spiritual intel-lect, truth	Despair, loneliness
Seventh	Crown of head	Violet	Divine wisdom, grace, connection to the divine	Spiritual depression, ego-centered spirituality

Learning how the chakras work allows us to pay greater attention to our divine energy. Working with the chakras, we can let sacred energy flow freely throughout our physical bodies, bringing us closer to merging our physical and spiritual lives in a state of harmony.

One of my first spiritual revelations was discovering the science of the chakra system. I clearly recall my first chakra meditation. With each chakra I focused on, I could feel more energy being pumped into my system. I could actually sense an inner cleansing taking place. I was touching the source of my own being. When you learn to work with your chakras, you not only reduce stress; you truly connect to a vibrant part of yourself. We have access to a more holistic approach to healing and health. And it's right inside of us.

Learning about divine energy and Interior Power means learning to work with your chakras. This energy system reflects and holds your energy, cycling it between your consciousness and your body. It envelops you with emotionally charged power created from life experiences, good and bad. This emotion-charged energy influences your physical body and mental and emotional health. Every thought and experience you have ever had has been filtered through and recorded in the cells of your chakra centers.

Every thought you have is recycled through the body by the chakra system. This is why it's essential to grasp the truth captured in the simple phrase *what you think, you create*. When you think with fear, fear runs through the body. You act out of fear and create situations that create more fear. The energy of fear creates chaos and anxiety for your whole being. Thinking with the energy of love, on the other hand, creates a healing vibration through the body.

Another issue for the chakras is balance. For our physical and spiritual natures to be in harmony, our lower chakras must be balanced with our upper chakras. In other words, our survival instincts and base emotions have to be brought into harmony with our higher emotions and spiritual focus. It's like the symbol of the yin-yang: the two energy fields must be balanced in order to create completeness. We will get more into this topic of balancing the higher self and the lower self in the next chapter on Inner Attunement. By learning to balance the forces of the chakra system, we can take better control of the energy within.

Energy Communication and Intuition

Since we are all living energy bodies, we are all susceptible to the energies of others. We all experience *energy communication* every day. Being around some people makes you feel good, and being around certain others can make you feel like you were hit by a New York taxicab. Your intuition zones in and shouts at you, "Get away — this guy's a creep!" or "Hey, she's cool — let's stick around." Nearly all of us are able to sense energies at this level.

You can practice this kind of energy communication by going to a party, bar, or club. The energy in these places can be a bit intense; at least it is for me. I tend to stay away from crowds. But you are likely to be able to test how you feel around a total stranger and begin to pay more attention to people's different energies. In her book *Anatomy of the Spirit*, Caroline Myss explains, "We are constantly 'in communication' with everything around us through this system [the chakras], which is a kind of conscious electricity that transmits and receives messages to and from other people's bodies. These messages from within the energy field are what intuitives perceive."*

There is a big difference between psychic abilities and intuition, but the two have similarities as well. Let me explain. Intuition is a skill that everyone has. It is one aspect of the voice of divine guidance that we talked about in the last chapter. Intuition keeps you on your path and promotes inner healing. Psychic abilities are much broader, reaching into the spiritual, mental, and cosmic dimensions. They include mediumship, clairvoyance, and prophecy. Psychic abilities are also a channel for Universal Knowledge. This is why I can look at you and see things you may not know at the time, or confirm what you do know. That's why I say everyone is intuitive, but not everyone is psychic. A person with strong intuitive powers may become a healer, spiritual teacher, or spiritual therapist, even if he or she isn't a psychic. I happen to be a psychic and a teacher, but not a healer. Even nonpsychics will get psychic flashes from time to time, but the voice of intuition is everyone's everlasting guide.

Intuition is the way the chakras communicate with you. The more you pay attention to how you feel in a situation or around people, the stronger you become at reading energy. The everyday mystic must know how to read energy and tell if it is positive or negative. The more you can feel negative energy, the less you want to be around it and the less you react to its life lessons. The more you steep yourself in the positive, the

---

* Myss, *Anatomy of the Spirit*, 33–34.

closer you get to following the mystic's path. And the great thing is, you will feel better. The way to tune yourself to your intuition is to pay attention to it. Go with your first gut instincts. The mortal mind will quickly come in with a "get-real" reaction, so act on that first whisper of the intuitive voice.

The Holy Spirit

We have all heard, in some form or fashion, about the Holy Spirit. In the South, where I was raised, they call it the Holy Ghost. I had my first encounter with the idea of the Holy Ghost when I was a young kid. I say *idea* because the Holy Spirit wasn't really there, and that's my point. I was attending a Southern Baptist tent revival. For those of you who are unfamiliar with this, you are not missing much. A revival is a day or weekend of lectures on hellfire and damnation. The purpose is to get you, the sinner, to be raised up by the Holy Ghost, walk up to the front of the tent, then let the preacher call you into the flock of the righteous. Praise Jesus! These revivals always happen outdoors, during the hottest part of summer. I think they choose that part of the year because the heat makes people delirious and more vulnerable to "salvation."

Well, being the little psychic kid I was, I watched these people who were supposedly being anointed by the Holy Ghost, expecting to see something. I was looking for this ghost everyone kept shouting about. By then I was pretty good at seeing and feeling things that most people couldn't see or feel. But there was nothing. I just saw people with pale faces full of fear going forth to be anointed, hoping to keep their butts out of hell and to secure their places in heaven.

In my opinion, the Holy Spirit has better things to do than keep us out of a hell that does not exist — such as keeping us out of the hells we create for ourselves. Through my research and psychic readings, I have learned that the Holy Spirit is alive and well in all of us. It doesn't descend from the heavens; it arises from our very beings.

The Holy Spirit is the divine breath of the gods. Its nature is feminine. For this reason, some have called this spirit Sophia, the Goddess of Wisdom. This breath of life is dwelling in all of us, though sometimes she is lying dormant. We just have to call forth her energy and begin to let it direct our lives and destinies.

The word *holy* means "whole," and *spirit* is equivalent to "being." So, the Holy Spirit can be thought of as a force pushing all existence toward wholeness. When this energy is called, it helps sustain, balance, and restore peace, bringing wholeness back to the individual or a situation. Mystics have worked with the Holy Spirit for centuries because it is a realized, potent force within them.

The challenge for you, in this stage of your growth, is to learn how to invoke the Holy Spirit to teach, protect, and guide you. The Holy Spirit is ready to be your guardian on the path. Some use prayer to invoke the spirit; some use meditation. I just quiet myself, take a deep breath, exhale, and say, "Come, Holy Spirit." It's that easy. You will be amazed at the release of negative energy when she is invoked. Deep, focused breathing is another way of calling forth the Holy Spirit. This works because the Holy Spirit is the breath of life. Try it. You will begin to feel sacred vibrations manifest within your body and your life.

Since the Holy Spirit is the balancer and the energy of

wholeness, you can use her for the purpose of healing, guidance, and protection. Every time I sit down to write, do a reading, teach, or perform a house blessing, I call for the light of the Holy Spirit. I just say, "Come, Holy Spirit," ask her to protect or bless the person, place, or thing, say thank you, and it's done.

Just remember that the Holy Spirit has a goddess nature and that her power is meant to be used wisely. Her energy is active only when it's called upon with pure intent. I never felt anything at the tent revival because at the revival, people were not called to salvation by love, but by fear; the Holy Spirit never answers a call when manipulation is the intent. If you try something like that, you are in for a cosmic slap in the face.

Begin to pay attention to energy, and you will activate its presence in your life. Learn to invoke the Holy Spirit, and you will create the vortex you need for integrating into your life the lessons in the following chapters.

Interior Power Prayer

Holy Spirit, come. Bring to me the Sacred Energy of the divine so that I may have Interior Power. This power is fueled by love, and it now washes over me. Every cell, every organ, and every bone are now activated by this sacred energy. I now put my intention on this positive power. May it direct my life to its fullest potential and guide me to my destiny.

I know that I control my thoughts, and I allow my Interior Power to enrich my mind. No longer will I fall into fear, but I will live in love. The Sacred Power that you, the divine, have bestowed upon me will activate pure intention and pure thought. May I now be a channel of this power to bless the world. With your blessing I now reclaim this power as my own and take it back from that which is no longer right or healthy for me. I accept this blessing here and now, and to you, divine presence in the universe, I say thank you.

Wisdom Tips for Interior Power

1. Read Caroline Myss's *Anatomy of the Spirit*. Everyone on the mystics' path should have this book. Caroline is the queen of energy medicine, and her book will really take you deeper into what she calls the science of subtle energy.

2. Begin to pay attention to — and follow — gut feelings and intuitive hunches.

3. Get to know the Holy Spirit. Always act out of pure intentions and love, and you will activate her presence in your life.

CHAPTER SIX

INNER ATTUNEMENT

You've probably heard the statement "The kingdom of heaven is within." In this chapter you will learn the skills you need to make this statement a reality in your life.

You create a peaceful "inner heaven" by working with the divine energy flowing in your body, the energy you discovered in the previous chapter. You control, balance, and tune this energy to bring clarity, calm, and heart-centered focus. This process of Inner Attunement allows you to maintain your interior power, strengthen your connection to the divine, and continue on the path of spiritual growth. It gives you a fresh wellspring of energy to invest in your life.

Inner Attunement is based on the daily practice of going within. The demands and stress of life make our minds run here and there, distracted with the business of everyday living. To overcome these distractions and live your life on a spiritual foundation, you must quiet your mind and become better acquainted with your inner life. And you have to work at it, day by day, which is why Inner Attunement is the dirt work of soul development. You must go deeper and deeper within, lifting one layer of consciousness after another. It's hard work, but the payoff is big: the further you dig, the more fertile your inner landscape becomes.

In my own life, I have found three attunement tools that help me attain, maintain, and retain my inner stamina and Sacred Energy: meditation, prayer, and guided imagery. All three work together very closely, and as I will explain below, they aren't necessarily separate from one another. Meditation calms and controls the mind. Prayer brings you into direct contact with the divine. Guided imagery creates positive mental pictures that help you access spiritual power.

Meditative Prayer

There is so much out on the market about meditation and prayer. Some teachers say there is an important difference between meditation and prayer, and some say there isn't. I'm one of those who thinks there isn't much difference between the two. What matters is the intent behind the practice. When your intent is spiritual communion and Inner Attunement, meditation and prayer really come together as one.

There is some truth to the saying that "Prayer is talking to God, and meditation is listening." But I think we should always be doing both when we go within, which is why I'm a believer in what I call *meditative prayer* (you could also call it *prayerful meditation*). Meditation is the science of calming and controlling the mind, and prayer brings about the actual communion between you and the divine. So, meditative prayer means calming the mind in order to connect with the divine through your soul. You quiet the mind's chatter, focus your intent on spiritual communion, and both talk to and listen to the divine presence. You can have other purposes, too — such as relaxation, self-healing, or even achieving prosperity — but you should always hold the intent of communion with the divine.

When I was a kid in church the only thing I really liked, besides seeing people get dunked underwater at the pool-pit, was closing my eyes in prayer. There was something sacred about it, even if the preacher was being long-winded. During those prayer times I could feel myself fall deep into peaceful darkness. For a few short moments I would step inside myself, following a pulling sensation. It was even better if the person leading the prayer was choosing positive words. I felt safe inside myself; it was just God and me, shut off from the world outside. I didn't fully understand what it meant to be closer to God, but I sure felt something stirring within me. Even then I was meditating with prayer. No one would have used the word *meditating* back then, but that's what it was.

I see so many people using meditation to get out of their reality or to distract themselves from their waking issues. That shouldn't be your purpose. You should use the practices of Inner Attunement to gain the inner strength you need to approach waking reality with inspiration, not to avoid it.

I'm often asked how long one should pray or meditate. I say do whatever feels right to you. The Gods really don't care, just as long as you do it. I don't think it is necessary to spend hours praying or meditating. When I'm on the road with a tour or doing a day full of readings, a few minutes of deep breathing with a prayerful intent works wonders. So, I usually tell people that five to ten minutes a day of meditative prayer can be enough. If you want to go longer, more power to you. I myself don't have the temperament to make it as a monk. But from time to time I do like a good forty-five-minute inner workout.

Staying Grounded

When you meditate or pray, it is important to be in your body. A lot of folks like to meditate to get out of their bodies. Stop it! Too much of that will make you ungrounded and basically air-headed. Prayer and meditation should be used to help you become more grounded in your body, not less.

After every prayer or meditation, I use a phrase or image to help me or my audience become grounded in the experience and come back with a feeling of physical security. You are doing no good for yourself or others if you stay in the clouds. This is why I'm critical of some of the astral projection books on the market — it's another popular psychic gimmick. Yes, astral projection is real, but it shouldn't be an immediate goal for most of us. If we can barely find our way in the physical realm, why are trying to float around in the astral? Stay on the earth, where the real work needs to be done. If the Gods wanted you in the astral realm, you'd already be dead and gone to the light for the next level of your mission.

You are in your body for a reason. So get over it and learn to love being alive and in your body. Here is an exercise for doing just that. This exercise is great when you are having one of those spacey days, or when you just need to commune with nature. Do it outside in a natural setting if possible. If you can't, the visualization is still powerful.

Grounding Exercise

Get comfortable and close your eyes. Call forth the energy and power of the Holy Spirit and let it surround you. Take three deep breaths. One . . . two . . . three.

Imagine that you are sitting against a sturdy, tall oak tree. You feel supported as your back rests gently against its bark. You look up into its canopy of thick emerald-colored leaves, as they blow gently with a soft breeze. Rays of sunlight shine through the leaves, making their way down to the top of your head and your shoulders.

Breathe in, feeling that you are becoming more secure and relaxed, and then exhale. Stress begins to dissipate. As you continue to breathe relaxed and easy, pay attention to the base of your spine. Feel the energy of your first chakra. Feel this base chakra root itself down into the earth you are sitting on. Like your friendly oak tree, you are rooting yourself back into the womb of Mother Earth. Breathe in again and allow yourself to merge, energetically, with the earth. Feeling the bright crimson of the root chakra piercing into the ground, winding around and in sync with the roots of the oak tree, take another breath.

You are feeling more secure in your body. You are feeling safe. Any stress and anxiety in your legs and lower back is now dissipating. As you breathe in and out, allow the stress to release into the earth and wash away, like a stream of cleansing water. Mother Earth will take the stressful energy and return it to you transformed, through your now-integrated energy roots. You are soaking up this divine earth energy through your root chakra.

Spiritual nutrients begin to metabolize within your lower energy centers. You breathe in earth power and exhale the stress and anxiety. A recycling and cleansing of power is taking place. Feel it as you breathe in, relaxed and easy.

You are still sitting quietly and comfortably against the oak tree, still feeling the gentle breeze and the warm sunlight. You are now grounded into the earth, rooted within the earth's womb. Repeat within your mind this affirmation: *I'm secure and safe in the world. I am the child of the Mother Earth. As above, so below.*

Breathe in...and out. When all the stress in your lower body is released and you feel secure, you can move your body around and open your eyes.

Clear Focus

The practices of Inner Attunement help you to achieve what I call *clear focus*. Clear focus is mental clarity, the kind of clear-headedness you feel after exercising or when you've released stress and anxiety in some other way. And behind the clear focus is a clear knowing that you are going to be all right. The more you go within and develop a spirit-directed conscious-ness, the more clear focus you begin to have, and the more open you are to guidance from your soul and positive strate-gies for moving forward. The outside world can really fog up your mind, and attuning to the inside world can help clear that fog.

Here is my version of an easy exercise I learned from a colleague of mine who was a spiritual healer. It helps bring about inner peace and clear focus. I use this practice when I'm feeling overwrought with stress and hitting a meltdown. When you are that bogged down, it's time to step back and take your power back and regain clarity. This exercise will help you to do just that. You can use it on a daily basis or as needed when your stress level is hitting the roof.

Inner Peace and Clarity Exercise

Close your eyes and take a few deep breaths. Imagine the light of the Holy Spirit around you. Put a hand on your forehead and say aloud or to yourself the words *peace to my mind, peace to my mind, peace to my mind.*

Take another deep breath, exhale, and put a hand on your chest, repeating the words *peace to my emotions, peace to my emotions, peace to my emotions.*

Take a deep breath and put a hand on your stomach and re-peat the words *peace to my body, peace to my body, peace to my body.*

Take another deep breath and relax. You will begin to feel anxiety fall away and your mind clear. Repeat the exercise as needed for full relaxation and clarity.

Heart Centeredness

As you become conscious of energy, power, and attunement, you must also learn to tap into the most powerful wellspring of Interior Power — the heart. The heart center, or fourth chakra, is where the higher self resides. It is also the alchemi-cal bridge between your physical, emotional, and spiritual aspects. Focusing on the heart, therefore, helps you achieve balance.

When I do my readings, I go straight for the heart. My higher self checks in with the client's higher self, and I get the scoop on just what they're challenged with emotionally and spiritually. I get insights on what is causing the imbalance in them and in their life. Anything out of sync can be detected in the heart, so that's where true healing and spiritual growth start.

A heart-centered approach increases the power of any spiritual practice, including meditation and prayer. I believe that when you pray for or send a blessing to someone, it is the heart that gives power to the thought. When you call the Holy Spirit, she comes to you through the heart. Focusing Inner Attunement practices in the heart creates an upwelling of sacred energy that can bring a sense of harmony.

Here is a simple exercise in guided imagery that helps you balance your emotions and become more heart centered in your life. You can repeat the exercise as many times as needed to relax and become fully centered in your heart chakra.

Heart-centering Exercise

Take a deep breath, and allow yourself to relax. Take another deep, cleansing breath and with the exhale call forth the light of the Holy Spirit and let it surround you. Place a hand in the middle of your chest.

Feel your heart beat with a rhythm all its own. Imagine within your chest a spinning wheel of green light. Breathe in the green light, inhale and exhale, allowing any anxiety to leave and stress to dissipate. Keep your hand on your chest and repeat aloud or to yourself the words *balance, peace, harmony.*

Still breathing with ease, you begin to feel those words vibrate in tune with your heartbeat. Those vibrations are now moving through your entire system. Take another deep breath in and then exhale, feeling your emotions balance and the stress releasing. When you are ready, open your eyes.

When talking about the heart, the topic of forgiveness can't be far behind. The inability to forgive, to let go of anger, is often the main reason people can't become fully centered in their hearts. Emotional power that comes from anger or fear can be like glue, clogging up the channels of your heart center. Letting anger and resentment fester in your heart is not exactly the best way of welcoming the Holy Spirit. It's not good for your emotional health or your spiritual health.

But most of us find forgiveness hard to deal with. I think that's because forgiveness means letting go of something in which we have invested a large amount of emotional energy. Someone somewhere has ticked you off and you have probably done the same to someone else. The specifics don't matter in the long run. What matters is that you are investing your sacred energy in the past, and it's not returning a very healthy profit back to you. Revisiting those memories just gets you ticked off over and over again and you become bitter.

Forgiveness does not mean saying, "Okay, everything is fine, I forgive you." Forgiveness is the conscious act of surrendering your anger — and the people or situations that created it — to the universe. In this act of letting go, you tell the universe, "Please take this; I am no longer giving it my energy. May your will be done." This last part has to do with karma. Trust me folks, everyone has karma time coming. The universe does not need you to be the karmic police squad. Everyone has to face the consequences of his or her actions at some point.

To promote forgiveness, I have tried that old exercise of writing names on a piece of paper and then burning it. I found myself not really letting go, but just wishing the actual people were burning in the flames! Now I use the guided-imagery forgiveness exercise that follows instead. It's a simple but powerful way of letting go and forgiving yourself and others, and it really works, at least for me. You might want to try it close to bedtime. While you sleep, the imagery will continue to cycle in your mind and heart, transforming the energy you are releasing. Your dreams may be really interesting after this exercise.

Forgiveness Exercise

Relax. Take three deep breaths, slow and steady. One...two...three. Close your eyes. You are surrounded by the power and energy of the Holy Spirit.

Picture in your mind a favorite outdoor place in nature — a grassy cliff overlooking the ocean, a forest glen, a vast range of land touching tall majestic mountains in the distance. Hear the sounds of the place — birds, waves, running water, rustling leaves. Smell the smells. You are sitting comfortably in this place, feeling safe and relaxed. Look up into the open blue sky. The sun is shining a brilliant gold, and you feel the warm rays cascade down onto your skin, touching your head and shoulders. Breathe in the warm air...and exhale.

You look around, and you see a wooden table in the distance. You walk over to it and see that there are some wooden cages, each holding a pure white dove. As you get closer, you notice names on the cages, the names of people who have caused you pain or wronged you in some way. One at a time, you focus on each name, bringing that person to the forefront of your mind and feeling the associated emotions.

Take a few deep breaths, relaxed and easy. Choose a cage and say the person's name. Open the cage door, and let the dove fly. Release it into the wide blue sky. See the dove and the bitter feelings connected to this particular person fly away and disappear into the sun. Breathe and say *let it go*.

Choose another cage. Say the name. Release its dove. See the dove and the bitter feelings connected to this person fly away and disappear into the sun. Breathe and say *let it go.*

Repeat the process until all the doves have been released. Take three deep breaths — one...two...three — and let it all go.

When you are ready, give thanks to your higher self for having the strength to let go. Remind yourself that you are better and stronger for having forgiven. Open your eyes, and feel lighter and more fluid and free.

Balancing the Higher and Lower Selves

In the previous chapter on Interior Power, you learned about the chakras and the body's energy anatomy. You learned that the lower three chakras, which are concerned with the physical plane, make up the lower self. And you learned that the upper four chakras, associated with the emotional and spiritual planes, are the seat of the higher self. An important part of Inner Attunement is balancing the needs and pulls of the lower self with the sacred intelligence of the higher self.

Both of these components of your being are necessary expressions of your individual personality. The lower, or ego, self is what allows you to focus on daily life in the physical plane, but it can be challenging. It will just run wild if you let it; it's like a monkey darting here and there, looking for anything that will satisfy its need for physical and emotional security. It's always looking to the outside for comfort. It is not linked to the soul as the higher self is. It can be touchy, dramatic, and critical. It carries with it all the aspects of negativity that you have been taught and have chosen to believe.

To have any hope of living your life on a spiritual foundation, your lower self has to come under the control of your higher self. Your higher self is the self-realized and individualized part of you, the part that is conscious of the fact that you are divine. It is the all-seeing eye of the soul, the seeker of mystical experience and unlimited potential.

The higher self should be the driving force of your life, the part of you that calls the shots. It should be projected through the lower self as actualized consciousness. This is what I mean by "balancing" the lower and higher selves. When in balance, the higher and lower selves work well together, manifesting the harmony of the physical and the spiritual.

The task is to bridge the chakras one to the next so that they can work together as a harmonious whole. When this happens, the higher self can take on its natural role as director of your consciousness, while the lower self happily concerns itself with things like hunger, sex, and security. The chakra-scan exercise that follows creates an inner space that can help you reach the goal of balance. It's a quickie version of a longer meditation. I recommend that you take ten to fifteen minutes out of your day to complete it. For deep attunement, you may want to do it at least three times a week. With your higher and lower selves balanced, you become not only a more self-realized and balanced person, but also a clearer channel for the divine.

Chakra–balancing Exercise

Find a quiet place. Relax, get comfortable, and close your eyes. Take three deep breaths, allowing yourself to go deeper with each exhale.

Let outside thoughts drift away as you shift your attention away from them. Call forth the light of the Holy Spirit to surround you.

Send your focus to the base of your spine and imagine a wheel of red, glowing light. As you see the ball of light begin to spin, breathe in the color red. And with the exhale let go of any tension you may feel here. Let it go. Say to yourself or aloud the word *peace*.

Let your attention move upward within your being to the area of your sex organs. Now the red wheel of light disappears in the distance and you see a spinning orange wheel of light. Breathe in the orange color, and with the exhale let go of any tension, stress, or fear you may feel here. Say the word *peace*.

Still relaxed and easy, move your attention up to the center of your stomach and let the spinning wheel of orange light fade away and be replaced by a yellow wheel of spinning light. You know what to do: breathe in the yellow, exhale the yellow, and release all tension. Say *peace*.

The yellow light spins away, and a green light begins spinning as you move your attention into the middle of your chest. Breathe in the green, letting it fill your entire chest cavity, and let it flow throughout your body as you exhale. This green energy vibration is bringing balance and calming unsettled emotions. Say *peace*.

As you feel relaxed and more vibrant, your attention enters the area of your throat. You see a blue spinning wheel of light come to the surface as the green wheel fades into the background. Breathe in the blue, exhale the blue, and move the neck around to give the energy room to spin and cycle. Let the stress dissipate, and say *peace*.

The blue vibration leaves your focus as you move your attention into the middle of your forehead. Now you begin to see a spinning wheel of indigo energy. Breathe in the indigo, exhale, and let any stress in this area go, as you say *peace*.

The indigo color introduces you to the area at the crown of your head. The indigo becomes lighter and turns into a wheel of spinning violet energy. Allow yourself to be consumed by this violet color; inhale and exhale it. It leaves you with a renewed feeling of connection and focus, which becomes even stronger as you say *peace*.

Now, focus on a sphere of white light shining above your head. It begins to move. It descends through the top of your head, past your forehead and throat, down through the chest and stomach, down through the sex organs, and comes to rest at the base of your spine. You see the red ball of light at the base of your spine merge with the white light. Take a deep breath. As you exhale, you begin to feel yourself grounded into this experience. Stress and tension have been washed away. You feel connected and attuned. When you are ready, open your eyes.

The basic truth of Inner Attunement is that the everyday mystic must have daily quiet time to practice attuning within. After a while you will begin to see that your mind will want its alone time, and prayer or meditation will come easily.

Inner Attunement Prayer

Divine presence in the universe, with this prayer I call forth your spirit. At this moment your energy wells up within my very being. I feel your sacred energy touch my soul. I know that by going within myself, I embrace the true meaning of the mystical life. The kingdom of heaven is within. The act of Inner Attunement washes my fears away.

I receive the blessing of attunement. I am balanced, I am healthy, and I am now truly alive. From this moment I begin to live life from the inside out. I am directed every step of the way by your guidance and advice, Holy Spirit. No more will I fear you, great spirit; I will love you, as you love me. I accept this blessing here and now. And I thank you.

Wisdom Tips for Inner Attunement

1. Create a daily prayerful meditation practice. A few minutes a day is fine.
2. Pay attention to your breathing. Deep, focused breathing will work wonders in promoting attunement.
3. Listen to some soothing music to help relax the mind and body.
4. Practice yoga or tai chi. They are great motivators of inner peace and can help you achieve Inner Attunement.

CHAPTER SEVEN

CONSCIOUS CREATION

We create our own reality. This statement has been one of the most popular — and misunderstood — teachings in the New Age movement. But the truth it expresses is fundamental to spiritual development.

I've had many people in my seminars ask how they can learn to create their own realities. This kind of question shows some confusion about the concept. You are always creating your reality. It's an inherent ability and a part of being human, so you don't have to learn how to do it. What most people *do* have to learn, however, is how to create the kind of inner and outer reality that keeps them on the path of spiritual growth.

We are creative beings, and our minds are powerful. What we create in our minds shapes our experience of the world, and even the world itself. It all hinges on perception — how you see yourself, your situations, and the world you are living in. A person who sees herself as a desirable and successful person in a world of opportunities is going to create around herself a reality that's very different from the reality of a person who thinks of himself as a failure in a world intent on beating him down. Your perception shapes your thinking, your thinking shapes the way you act, the way you act affects the people around you — and it all gets reflected back at you.

Here's an example. Let's say you get up one morning, go to your coffeemaker and find that it's dead. No light is on, the burner is cold, and the water doesn't drip. You are faced with a choice. You can perceive the coffeemaker's death as a bad omen, because it is Monday morning and it's raining outside. You can rant and rave as you get dressed and think the day is going to be as dysfunctional as the coffeepot. If you do, you have already created the day's reality, and you haven't even gotten to work! You will be in a dark mood, and people will treat you accordingly. You will expect the worst, and the worst will likely happen. Or, you can make a very different choice. You can see the dead coffeemaker as an excuse to change your routine and stop to get a latte on the way to work. You can see it as a good reason to go to the mall and buy the new coffeemaker you've been eyeing for weeks. The coffeemaker's demise becomes an opportunity. You make this choice with positive energy, and the positive energy is projected into the world. You are happy, and people treat you as someone they want to interact with. Your day goes great, and you get to try your new coffeemaker the next morning.

This is a simple example, but the same principle applies for life's bigger challenges and traumas. Thought is action, and it manifests itself in you and your world. Most important, you have the power to *choose* how you will think and perceive.

You decide what type of power you use to fuel and project your thoughts. It's as simple as that — a matter of learning to direct your thought patterns in constructive and positive ways, to consciously create your reality.

Spiritual Self-reliance

For me, learning this truth was an incredible revelation that helped me transform my life. I realized that I could not be responsible for anyone's thoughts but my own. That in itself was a great relief. And if I didn't like my life, then I could change it by changing my thoughts and perception about it. I could no longer blame anyone else for my misery. After a while we all come to the same realization: the only burden we are carrying is that of the reality we have created for ourselves. We must take responsibility for our actions, thoughts, and feelings. Self-reliance, therefore, is the first rule of Conscious Creation.

This is a spiritual principle as much as a psychological one. Not only can you make your life better through Conscious Creation of your reality; there is a spiritual source within yourself that will support you in doing it. Conscious Creation is a matter of making choices about manipulating and accessing Interior Power, or Sacred Energy. You are your own energy source, and you can be aligned with divine energy — or not.

In other words, Conscious Creation is important not only for creating happiness and positive outcomes, but also for making contact with the divine and expanding the presence of the sacred within you. The divine is the universal force of creation. When we create consciously, with divine inspiration, we become partners with the divine. We become cocreators. This insight was explored by the mystic and psychic Edgar Cayce. As explained by Herbert Puryear in his book *The Edgar Cayce Primer*, Cayce's ideas about cocreation "define us as souls with the attributes of spirit, mind and will. At this spiritual level, the mind is the aspect of our being which enables us to be cocreators with God."*

Cayce meant that our Interior Power is an extension of the creative force of the universe. By using our Interior Power consciously, to realize intentions of love, we become channels for universal sacred energy. This alchemical energy, vibrating with love, is the creative force of the Gods — the life force. When we project it into the world with our thoughts, we act as the agents of the Gods.

Spiritual Responsibility

The power we have as creators of reality gives us tremendous responsibility. We can infuse the creative energy of thought with the power of love and use it for constructive purposes, or we can infuse it with the power of fear and use it for destructive purposes. Building reality with the energy of fear will cause chaos and pain, whereas using the true essence of love leads to limitless creative potential. Thinking with love allows you to have a new coffeemaker in the morning and invites the Holy Spirit to manifest itself.

Your mind thinks the thoughts that create your reality, but it also chooses what those thoughts will be. It can do both at

---

* Herbert B. Puryear, PhD, *The Edgar Cayce Primer: Discovering the Path to Self-Transformation* (New York: Bantam, 1982), 59.

the same time because it isn't just one mind. Remember the distinction I made earlier about the mortal mind and the mystical mind? Well, that's helpful for understanding the choices involved in spiritual responsibility.

The mortal mind is good at solving math problems, but only the mystical mind can find solutions to spiritual problems. The mystical mind has the ability to create and direct with love. The mortal mind is more apt to do the opposite because it's not even buying this "we create our own reality" bit. You see? Both aspects of your mind are needed, but you must choose which one is going to direct your life and thoughts. In order for the two to work as one, the mystical mind must start directing the play going on in your mind. The mortal mind follows and takes care of all the details of everyday living. You learn this power of mindfulness by watching how you think and what you say, and changing the negatives to positives.

For example, there is probably someone in your life who has caused you lots of pain. You can go with the knee-jerk, fear-based reaction of the mortal mind and direct thoughts of hate toward that person. You can wish bad things upon him. Or, you can acknowledge your feelings but turn them around toward the positive. You can think, "I don't really like so-and-so, but may God love him." The energy you project toward the person is transformed. Instead of a curse, you have created a blessing.

Making this into a habit of mind takes a lot of work. But with a steady practice of *re-minding* yourself, you can do it. Your mind has already started the alchemical process of rewiring itself because you've read this far into this book.

You breathe life into your thoughts, and how much life you give them is up to you. As an everyday mystic you learn that breathing your life force into fearfulness is not helping your spiritual growth. Negative thoughts projected toward other people are bad for them, but they are even worse for you. It's a law of the Gods: what you send out, you get back. Yes, it's called karma. You reap what you sow.

Releasing Negative Thought-forms

Negative beliefs, attitudes, and perceptions lead to emotions of anger, hate, and depression. These emotions reinforce the thinking that caused them in the first place. The negative thinking becomes so strong that it takes over your consciousness. It becomes a thought-form, as real as this book, like a wall around your heart. It separates you from other people and stifles love.

Negative thought-forms reinforced by negativity over a long period of time can develop an evil energy of their own and even take on a personality. To me, psychically, they look like blobs of dark energy in a person's aura or swirling tornadoes bouncing here and there within the energy field of the body. The more you feed a negative thought-form with negative energy, the more hold it has on your unconscious, making you ungrounded, depressed, and ill. Eventually, it will possess you. A client dealing with a powerful negative thought-form looks to me like a tied-up ball of dark twine, unable to move, energetically paralyzed.

The good thing is, you have just as much power to project the positive as you do to project the negative. I have found that negative thought-forms must be fed constantly or they die. To stop feeding your negative thought-forms, you just have to become conscious of what you are thinking and change it to the positive. A sure way to begin changing the mind is to get in the habit of catching your thoughts. Catching your thoughts means grabbing them before they get projected out. It's as easy — and as hard — as thinking "damn you!" and then turning it around to "bless you" before you say it or allow it to circulate in your mind.

Another way to consciously confront the inner demons of your negative thought-forms is to use the power of prayer, in league with the Holy Spirit. When said aloud, the prayer that follows can invoke the divine assistance you may need to break the habit of feeding a negative thought-form.

Freedom from Negativity Prayer

Divine Holy Spirit, I am surrounded by your vibration and power. Help me to see clearly in my own life the light that shines from within. Your power and grace dissolve all negativity and release me from its grip. Your light shines forth, and all that lies in darkness is revealed. Through my conscious will, I no longer feed negativity. I stand on a spiritual foundation with pure intent. Amen.

Free Will and Destiny

Talking about the choices we make brings us to the question of free will versus destiny. Do we have the power to determine the courses of our lives, or are they scripted in advance by the Gods? This is an important question, but the answer doesn't really matter. Whether or not you believe in some kind of pre-destination, everything I've said so far in this chapter points to one conclusion: you have to live, think, and act as if the responsibility for your life is completely in your hands.

The ability to make conscious choices about the thoughts we create and the energy we project is one of the most important of our divine gifts. This is what is meant by the term *free will*. If you have a destiny, it is to exercise your free will, to create your reality consciously. Divine will speaks through your higher self and directs you to make choices that will keep you in harmony with the flow of creative energy in the universe. It is not asking you to conform to a divine agenda with a set of rights and wrongs. We are all entitled to experience divine richness and harmony, and Conscious Creation is the means of realizing that entitlement.

Yes, life hands us some pretty miserable stuff sometimes. A loved one dies; you wreck your car; your partner leaves you; you lose your job. But you can choose to see tragedies and difficulties as part of a never-ending struggle or as a series of challenges to face and overcome. This is the essence of free will.

Whatever you choose, you still have unique life lessons to learn. Having free will does not mean you can skip out on those lessons. The Gods know your spiritual curriculum and the excuses you may use to miss class. They will meet you at every corner until you face your issues. They won't punish you, but from time to time they will try to get your attention.

There is a power within you so great that it has gotten you this far. You are now at a point where you can choose a different way of living and thinking. You can listen to your higher self and begin right now to make a life worth living. The question you have to ask yourself over and over is "how am I using my free will?" Some choices cut you off from sacred energy, and some enhance its vibration within you. You must learn the difference. If you see that one choice leads to a bad situation, choose again. The more you come out of negative situations without getting stuck in them, the more you become a conscious cocreator.

Edgar Cayce has given us a simple three-part formula you can use to remember the basics of Conscious Creation: "The Spirit is the life, the Mind is the builder, and the Physical is the result."* *The Spirit is the life* means that in giving us the gifts of free will and the higher self, the divine presence has provided the foundation of Conscious Creation. *The Mind is the builder* means that your attitudes and thought-forms have creative power in your life and in the world. *The physical is the result* means that what you think manifests itself in the physical realm.

Conscious Creation Prayer

Divine presence, I surrender to you my mind. May your spirit fill me with an abundance of love, that I may think clearly. May Divine Spirit bless every thought I think with pure intent and bestow upon me the attitude of loving creation. I no longer give my thoughts to fear; I no longer react with anger. Love is the healing balm for my mind.

Oh, Holy Spirit, cast your light on the shadows that bind my ability to create a peaceful life with you. I see the light, the love, and the harmony, and I create my life with joy. Through the act of right thinking, the power of love

---

* Puryear, *The Edgar Cayce Primer,* 57.

infuses every thought with passion and truth, and from this, miracles begin to happen. With this blessing through the power of my intention, I give thanks.

Wisdom Tips for Conscious Creation

1. Remember that you are a channel for a divine creative force.
2. Know that with great power comes great responsibility.
3. Catch your thoughts, transforming them from negative to positive, and control your projections.
4. Think with love, not fear.

CHAPTER EIGHT

WHOLISTIC LIVING

*T*hroughout the previous chapters I have focused on the inner life of soul development. You have learned that inner attention, when focused correctly, develops your capacities for self-knowledge and communion with the divine. Now it is time to express those spiritual dynamics outward — to create a lifestyle aligned with your renewed sense of being. In this way, you become a clear channel of divine expression.

Merging the Physical and Spiritual Realms

As you explore your inner landscape, you become more in tune with the spiritual world. At the same time, you are living in the physical world. Straddling the two worlds is necessary for soul development, but the task of the everyday mystic is to bring the two together into what I call a *Wholistic* lifestyle.

When you have integrated the spiritual with the everyday, your social networks, relationships, and daily activities are all expressions of your inner light.

You may find that a Wholistic lifestyle develops naturally as you grow spiritually. As you start to think like a mystic — catching your negative thoughts, seeing the divine spirit in everything, developing a rapport with your soul — you begin bridging the two halves of your existence. You allow your spirit, the part of you in touch with the divine, to direct your life. Sacred energy guides your thoughts, your choices, and your experience. Your daily life is slowly transformed.

We've covered a lot of ground in the previous chapters, so this may be a good time to retrace your steps and review what you've learned. As you begin to express in your outer life the wisdom of the mystic's path, you want to be fully aware of what that wisdom is. As a reminder, here are some of the most important qualities of an everyday mystic:

1. You see the divine presence in everything. You accept the fact that you are a child of the divine and you know there are uncharted worlds to explore within and without.

2. You are increasingly aware of what distracts you from the light of the divine. You have learned to separate yourself from people, places, and things that sap your interior power. You know how to take your power back and reclaim your life.

3. Your higher self watches how you think. You catch your negative thoughts and transform them into the positive, even if you don't feel like being

positive. You always honor your feelings, but you don't let them overtake you.

4. You are accustomed to invoking Interior Power and spiritual guidance. You know that intuition, the Holy Spirit, spirit guides, and angels are there to offer their support, and you can hear their voices. You know there is a divine power guiding your every step.

5. You reserve quiet time for meditation and prayer, and you pay attention to your inner life.

6. You allow "gifts of the spirit" to come as they may. Your intent is not to develop your "psychic powers," and you avoid the psychic glamour factory.

7. You live with an inner calm, knowing that the everyday mystic has the privilege of seeing beyond the illusions of the physical world.

You won't *always* be able to express these qualities. Putting them into action is not always going to be like a day at Disney World. But as you live this spiritual wisdom, bringing the spiritual into every aspect of your physical life, you will find it becoming more and more a part of your being.

Being a Conduit of Divine Expression

Once you establish a bond with the divine, you are meant to express that divinity, to become a channel of peace and to share your light with others. It's no good to learn deeper wisdom and keep it for yourself; you must allow that wisdom to flow through you and illuminate those around you. I don't mean you should go out and preach to people, or become a medium and channel archangels. I'm speaking of being a channel or conduit of spiritual light just by being you, the real you in sync with your higher self. If every person on this planet took that one step into higher consciousness, the world would blink into total balance and peace in an instant.

When the divine is able to show itself through you, that very quality will influence those around you. You don't have to say a word. People will see the mystic in you just by your actions. We all know when we see a person who is "with it." Such a person carries an energy that's attractive and positive. We want to be around him or her. We want to know why he or she seems so at ease. What does this person know that we don't? Such people are often undercover mystics, tapped into a divine source that they have relied on for a long time. They affect people around them without preaching any specific beliefs. By being living examples of spiritual wholeness, such people help others find their way out of the dark and into the light. You can do the same.

Being a Force for Good in the World

Affecting people around you is one thing, but actively working for change should also be part of a Wholistic lifestyle. As mystics, we can't sit around with our spiritual knowledge and watch our planet fall apart. In addition to expressing our own personal light, we must help movements that use our collective light to help change the world.

An everyday mystic works to end the suffering, hunger, war, and injustice that exist in the world. He or she tries to reverse the ongoing destruction of the earth's ecosystems. This visionary action can take many forms. You can champion causes that work for peace and justice. You can get involved in charity work, contribute to human and animal rights organizations, and reduce your personal impact on the environment by consuming less and cutting back on your driving. You can take a stand in your own community and find ways to improve things right in your own backyard. If we all establish "light consciousness" in our own communities, we create ripples of change that will eventually become a wave of higher consciousness that washes over the land. Visionary action means looking at the whole picture and choosing how to make real change on the ground. There are mystics in every walk of life who use Interior Power to transform injustice, hate, and ignorance into love, peace, and sisterhood and brotherhood.

I feel like I should break out into singing "We Are the World." That may sound a bit sappy, but we *are* the world. One by one, spiritually enlightened people from all races and religions can band together and change fear and hate into love. I know this kind of thinking seems like a pie-in-the-sky dream. But remember the power of positive thinking and our ability to shape reality with our minds. If all human beings held in their minds one loving thought at the same time, this planet would never be the same. In the meantime, those of us with Interior Power need to do the right thing simply because we know everything is connected by divine oneness.

Reclaiming the Divine Feminine

When I was young I had many dreams in which I was visited by a woman dressed in Egyptian clothing, like the Goddess

Isis. In my visions we would walk on a beach or sit under an oak tree, and I'd tell her my troubles or concerns. She would help me see a better perspective. I felt safe with her. I realized that the Mother God, the divine feminine, was looking out for me. My own feminine principle was emerging within me and creating much-needed balance in my life.

I believe that a similar kind of balance between the masculine and feminine principles needs to happen in the world today. For the last couple of thousand years, organized religions have put a very masculine face on God and spirituality. This has helped make masculine energy dominant — and masculine energy has a dark side that brings about competitiveness, war, and the need for power. We can clearly see which of the energies has long been the driving force on this planet. However, before the rise of "God the Father," goddess worship was the norm. The qualities of intuition, compassion, and integrity were highly valued, and this was reflected in systems of thought. Feminine energy was strong, and people were more in touch with nature than they are today.

Why is this an issue for everyday mystics seeking to express their divine natures in the outer world? It's because the divine feminine is the lost piece of the puzzle of creating peace in the world. We need to recognize the divine feminine energy within ourselves and then bring this energy into the way we live our lives and work for change in the world. A big part of Wholistic Living is recognizing the need for balance in the universe, and the Goddess is the catalyst for creating that balance.

As mystics we must move toward a more Wholistic view of the divine by bringing back the lost aspect of the divine feminine. Within us, our very souls are a mixture of masculine and feminine qualities. The feminine side has been stifled for a long time, but it is reemerging. I believe that the wave of higher consciousness upwelling globally is a result of many taking a more feminine approach to spirituality and life. Many of us are striving to live more in touch with feminine energies, and in doing so we are progressing toward a goddess-like perception of the divine. This doesn't mean the Goddess is replacing — or should replace — God. The Goddess is part of the One Source, the divine being; she is just one of the many faces of the divine.

I truly believe that if we are to create peace in the world and make it a better place for future generations we must accept that there is a Goddess, a divine feminine aspect to our spiritual natures. When this feminine energy comes alive in the hearts of men and women, it will bring harmony between the masculine and feminine principles in the universe, as well as within us.

Creating Soul Friendships

As we progress on our spiritual paths and embody the life of the mystic, we find ourselves letting go of people who are not healthy for us. During this process of letting go, it can feel like we are alone in the world. At times it's a challenge to be on the spiritual path and find people that share your ideals and passions. The good news is, your soul will attract others with like souls. The more you learn to live from within, the more you attract people into your life who strive for the same goal.

With all the ups and downs that life can spring on us, nothing is more soothing than having a network of friends you can count on, friends who share your spiritual values.

Sure, you work out your personal spiritual life alone between you and the divine being, but you need like-minded friends to help you keep going and to remind you of your potentials. You are strengthened by their embrace. I am blessed to have that kind of a network to lean on when I need it.

The farther you progress along your spiritual path, the more likely you are to meet people who don't just share your values and goals, but who also resonate with you 100 percent. They are cut from the same cosmic cloth. You feel like you have known them for a thousand years, and you can't conceive of them not being in your life. I call such people soul friends. I believe that your relationships with your soul friends were written into your personal life-chart long ago and that you are destined to meet them. But of course you don't have to share this belief to experience the magic of having soul friends.

Everyone has a story about the creation of a close friendship. I have talked to many people who felt they were led by some force or synchronicity to meet or "accidentally" meet people who have become important parts of their lives. The way I met the singer Jane Olivor is a good example. It all began with me buying one of her CDs some years ago. Then, through a series of synchronicities, I met with her after a concert, and a connection was born. After talking a bit, we realized we had many of the same interests. We both felt as if we already knew each other. We agreed we would keep in touch. I went to visit her in Maryland, and when I walked into the place where we were going to have lunch, Jane gasped, "That's it!" I asked her what she meant. "The symbol you are wearing!" She pointed to an unusual silver pendant around my neck that had a Star of David and a cross on it. "A psychic told me I would meet a young man and that that symbol would be involved. You're him!" For me, this was a confirmation from the Gods that a soul friendship had been activated.

Every time you meet someone, it's for a purpose. Your connections with people can lead not only to friendships but also to working relationships that raise the consciousness of both of you. This is the real purpose of relationships of any kind. Always pay attention to what relationships destiny brings you, good or bad. There is an avenue for soul growth in every life situation. To this day, I feel a psychic surge run through my system anytime I feel destiny is afoot. It's my cue from the Gods to pay attention. It amazes me every time I think about the divine orchestration that goes on behind the spiritual life.

Cultivating Holy Relationships

Throughout my professional career as a psychic I have noticed that many of the questions people ask me concern relationships — familial, platonic, or romantic. This isn't surprising, since relationships are such important parts of our lives. A "holy" relationship can be a dynamic catalyst in your soul development. In contrast, a difficult relationship can be a source of angst that blocks your connection with the divine. So having healthy, conscious relationships is particularly important for developing a Wholistic lifestyle.

I can't claim to be an expert on relationships — and God knows enough has already been written on the subject — but I have learned some important things about the spiritual aspects of relationships and how they relate to the goal of bringing your spiritual and physical lives together.

Relationships, of course, are about love. Love is a diverse

and multifaceted power, the glue that connects everything in the universe. One of the most important things to know about love is that it manifests itself in different ways among us humans. The ancient Greeks had a very helpful way of describing the different manifestations of love. They believed that love expressed itself as three different archetypal energies: Agape, Philia, and Eros. These archetypal energies create and sustain our relationships, allowing them to develop into whatever form they are destined to take. Being aware of the three types of love can help you become more conscious in your relationships.

Eros is the love energy that has inspired much of the passion in romance books, paintings, and movies. This energy stokes the fires of sexuality and erotic imagination. Everyone has felt a primal physical attraction to someone; this chemistry is the onset of Eros. Eros is often the energy that first connects us with others. If a person appears handsome or beautiful in our eyes, then Eros touches us. Eros by itself is not a strong enough foundation for a long-term relationship, and it has a dark side: you can be addicted to its power, striving only for physical pleasure without a deeper connection.

The archetypal energy of Philia resonates with a more tribal focus. It is the basis of friendships, loyalty, love for one's work, and pride. It is sisterly and brotherly love. It is easy to see that many of your friends and acquaintances are connected to you through this energy. The energy of Philia is very secure and not as fleeting as that of Eros. It can last forever and be very supportive. A downside of Philia is that it is conditional, which allows it to be used for the purpose of control. It can be used to foster guilt and divisive patriotism, and it can create exclusive in-groups such as the cliques many of us have experienced at work and in school.

The ultimate love in relationships is Agape, or spiritual love. Agape resonates to the love that God has for us. It is what makes a relationship holy. It creates a soul connection that goes beyond Eros and Philia. Agape love is unconditional; it does not ask for anything in return. Soul friends are bonded by Agape.

When you understand these energies, you can recognize when each of them comes into play in a relationship. Knowing and feeling the differences between them can help you decipher what type of relationship you are having with a person. A common source of difficulty in a relationship is one person feeling Eros while the other person feels only Philia in return. The best foundation for a relationship, romantic or platonic, is symmetry — both people feeling the same types of love toward each other. I have a few friendships that are bonded by both Philia and Agape. A conscious romantic relationship is energized with mutual Agape, Philia, and Eros. You have the soul and spiritual connection, the sexuality and passion, and the strong friendship. All three energetic ingredients make the relationship whole — and holy.

Wholistic Living Prayer

Holy Spirit, grant me the reward of living from my highest nature. I pray that you direct my life and steer the reins to keep me on the road to higher knowing. I know that you will give me the power of discernment and all illusion will be wiped away. I will live only in truth.

My life is blessed by your holy grace. I grow closer to you by living from spirit. Divine ones surround me with synchronicity that I might follow the steps that lead to my destiny. I now embody sacred virtue and reclaim its power. I accept this blessing and give thanks to thee, Holy Spirit.

Wisdom Tips for Holistic Living

1. Being an everyday mystic is a daily practice. Keep it up.
2. Pay attention to life situations. Destiny may be afoot.
3. Let go of fear. Life was meant to be lived with love.
4. Take action. Get involved in programs that can make a positive change for the planet.
5. Listen to your inner knowing to seek out and cultivate soul friendships and holy relationships.

CHAPTER NINE

ONENESS

*E*verything you have read in this book has pointed you toward a single goal: to be at one with yourself, the divine presence, and everything around you. This is the experience of *Oneness*, of being completely in sync with the sacred energy of the universe. Oneness happens when the real you, your higher self, is fully present at every moment, when your mind, body, emotions, soul, spirit, and psyche are all in unison with the divine.

The greatest barrier to Oneness is our tendency to dwell in the past and anticipate the future. No matter how much spiritual wisdom you've accumulated, you can't experience Oneness unless you are fully in the present. That's why the words *be in the present* are so powerful. The act of paying attention to what is going on now is what activates and makes possible everything you have learned so far. In essence, living the spiritual life is living in the present moment. Divine guidance, inspiration, Conscious Creation, and Oneness are all born from the now.

"The Power of Now"

We all have trouble being in the present, even when we try to make it our goal. Most of us spend much of our time — more than 80 percent of it, judging from my clients — directing our thoughts and energy toward people and events in the past and in the future. According to the spiritual teacher Eckhart Tolle, "[T]he compulsion to live almost exclusively through memory and anticipation...creates an endless preoccupation with past and future and an unwillingness to honor and acknowledge the present moment and allow it to be."*

The practical realities of today's world push you in the direction of living through "memory and anticipation," but there's no particular reason why you shouldn't be able to be fully in the present most of the time and experience Oneness regularly. The possibility of Oneness is open to you all the time. You just have to remember this fact and identify what's removing you from the present. Whatever it is — worry, guilt, anticipation, expectations, bitterness, anger — it's disconnecting you from the divine presence and blocking the possibility of Oneness.

An experience I had a short time ago is a good example of how easily we can get disconnected — and how it's possible

---

* Eckhart Tolle, *The Power of Now: A Guide to Spiritual Enlightenment* (Novato, CA: New World Library, 1999), 40.

to get back into the present and experience the power of One-ness. I was in Los Angeles to attend business meetings and a conference. Things started off poorly when I received a call on my cell phone as I walked into my hotel room. My two business meetings had been canceled. *Damn*, I thought. I had prepped very intensely for these meetings and invested a lot of my energy in the outcome. *Well*, I thought, *at least I have the conference to look forward to*. I had waited a long time to see in action the author who was speaking there, and his publisher had invited me to attend the sell-out extravaganza. I got in my rented car and plugged the destination data — just as I had it from the conference folks — into the electronic contraption that was supposed to tell me how to get there.

I followed its directions but soon realized that I was get-ting farther out of the city, away from downtown where the conference center was. I could feel the fire of irritation jump-ing up in me like a popcorn kernel in a hot oiled pan. There's nothing I hate more than getting excited about something and then seeing the potential of it falling apart. I could feel myself unraveling as I drove around a not-so-desirable part of Los Angeles, completely lost. With the car doors locked and my cell phone in hand, ready to dial 911 in case a ruthless street gang attacked me, I decided to give up on the conference. I was an hour late by that time and lost not only in Los Angeles but also in my mind. I was loaded with unhappy energy, thinking the whole trip had been a waste of time.

I plugged in the address of one of my favorite places in Los Angeles, the Bodhi Tree, a popular metaphysical book-store on Melrose Avenue in West Hollywood. The electronic travel director was not in my good graces, but it redeemed itself with a direct route to the Bodhi Tree. I easily found a parking space close to the bookstore, but I was still in a sour mood. I didn't feel at all like practicing what I always preach; I wanted to be miserable. I walked into the bookstore with my hands on my hips in a huff. A young lady behind the counter welcomed me, and I smirked a half smile. I looked around at the wonderfully packed bookstore and realized that I was in a safe place; bookstores always comfort me. I scanned the shelves, looking at books on reincarnation and spiritual enlightenment. On the walls, pictures of various saints and gurus — who probably would have handled the weekend better than I was — looked down at me. I could feel myself relax. As I turned around to enter another room in the store I heard a book fall. *Oh, gee*, I thought, *this is original — the old book-falling-off-the-shelf bit*. I looked around and saw the book that was on the floor. It was called *The Power of Now*, by Eckhart Tolle. "Uh huh," I said out loud, as I looked up to the heavens. "I hear you." I hadn't been in the now all weekend. I realized that if I didn't learn to go with the flow of events, I was in for a stressed-out career and personal life. I sighed with relief. (On another cosmic note, I think the Gods had a second message for me during this experience: New World Library, the publisher of *The Power of Now*, would later become my publisher. Don't you just love Destiny?)

After the experience at the bookstore, I decided to drive down the Pacific Coast Highway and think. I was relaxed enough to realize what an idiot I was for making this entire trip a disaster. I had only myself to blame. I knew better than this... or did I? I had spent most of the weekend invested in the future and not in the present. The meetings and the conference were supposed to happen, and they hadn't, and that had completely disconnected me from my higher self and the divine source.

I stopped off at a beach in Malibu. It was dusk, and the sun began to meet the ocean, a perfect marriage. It was stunning. I noticed a beautifully tanned and toned surfer afloat in the water, sitting peacefully on his surfboard. He smiled and motioned me to look out to sea. I scanned the ocean where he pointed. Right there before my eyes were seven or eight dolphins and a couple of golden seals, all playing with each other in the waves. I took off my shoes and rolled up my pants and waded in. I didn't know what I was going to do, but I wanted to be closer.

I looked around for the handsome surfer dude, but he was gone. I looked down and saw that I was waist-deep in water, and for a moment my mind seized on the idea of sharks. I turned to head back to the beach but stopped in midstep when I head the call of one of the dolphins. *Okay, you're right*, I thought. *Cut the fear crap.* I stood there and decided to let the salt water cleanse my fear and the negative residue of the weekend's mishaps from me. I watched the sea animals play. They weren't trapped by time or meetings or anything of that nature. They were right here, right now. They were living in a natural state of Oneness with life, God, and nature. The reality of Oneness expanded into my mind and engulfed me. I was one with the ocean, the dolphins, and the seals, completely in the present. We were all at a cosmic playground in the ocean of life. Leave it to nature to make a point. After the dolphins swam away into the horizon, I realized that even though my life was sometimes hectic and time sensitive, I could still be at one with myself and everything around me. I walked back to the beach, wet and filled with inner peace.

A Formula for Connecting

When I was pondering writing this chapter, a spiritual formula came to me: "let the past die; let the future unfold; live in the present moment." When I heard these words in my head, I was filled with energy. The formula was simple, but it captured the essence of what's involved in removing the barriers to Oneness. I think it will help activate this lesson for you, help your mind absorb it, and help the rest of your being embody it. Let's look at each part individually.

"Let the past die." The word *die* is the key word in this first part of the formula. Folks often say, "let the past go," but I think you have to do more than that. If you just let the past go, you just stop paying attention to it, for now. You let it hang out in a little storeroom in your mind, ready to come back and take you away from the present. For some reason we want to keep the past just near enough to fall back on. Instead, when you let the past die, you refuse to feed it your thoughts and energy. You starve it to death, and it can't come back to bother you.

"Let the future unfold." The future is in a continuous process of unfolding into the present. The message of this second phrase in our formula is to allow this to happen. Let yourself go with the flow and receive what's constantly coming into the present from the future, upstream. Trying to influence the future takes you out of the present, but that's only part of the problem. Giving attention to the future risks creating it from fear, whereas allowing the future to unfold by itself allows it to be created from love. Love is the force from which your future should be conceived. Walk into your future every day with love.

"Live in the present moment." If you allow the first two parts of the formula to take effect in your life, living in the present moment becomes easy. If you don't allow your energy to be stuck in the past or thrown into the future, it stays with you in the present, making possible the joy and fulfillment of Oneness.

Limitless Time

For Eckhart Tolle, the tendency to be preoccupied with the past and future is like being "trapped in time."[*] This rings true for me, and I have a feeling it does for you too. When you think about it, being too concerned with time is what takes us out of the present. We are all wrapped up in our schedules and planning for future events. We are constantly worried about "wasting" our time, as if it were a resource in short supply. We worry about how "fast" time seems to be passing.

But time doesn't have to be a trap. We can experience time without any barriers at all, as what I call *limitless time*. Limitless time is the essence of Oneness. It's when awareness of time disappears, almost as if you are outside of time. We all experience limitless time in our lives. For example, we all have moments of euphoria, or "peak experiences," when we feel connected to something larger than ourselves and all our juices are flowing, when we are completely "in the groove." Another type of limitless-time experience can happen during meditation or prayer. Many times, I've had the experience of going deep into meditative prayer and then coming out of it an hour later, after what seemed like both an instant and an eternity. The dream state can also be a form of limitless time.

---

[*] Tolle, *The Power of Now*, 40.

With practice, you can enter limitless time by choice. Your soul lives in limitless time and understands it completely. It's just a matter of making the mortal mind let go. Remind yourself to let the past die, let the future unfold, and live in the present moment. Know that within you there are no time constraints, jut Oneness every moment.

I'm not saying that you should ignore the physical world and your responsibilities. You don't have call up your boss and say, "I'm in the now, and you're not part of it." Be sensible. You can use human time to work and take care of business, but then after you have handled the practical situations, come right back into limitless time. You continue to work with human time but are not enslaved by its mental limits.

To conclude this chapter, I offer you the following Oneness Meditation. May it help guide you to the now.

Oneness Meditation

Make yourself comfortable. Take three deep breaths. Feel your mind and body become more relaxed and calm. Bring your attention within as you close your eyes.

You are still breathing, relaxed and easy. Now, say to yourself, *I am surrounded by the light of the Holy Spirit, and I am safe. Peace to my mind, body, emotions, and spirit.*

The stage is set. Now let's enter into the meditation.

Within your mind, visualize a place that is special and sacred to you, where you feel safe and secure. It can be a grassy glen surrounded by a thick, green forest; a warm beach, fresh with the scent of salty sea air; or a cozy plush chair in front of a crackling fire. Wherever you want to be, create it now, a safe place that's all your own.

As you get comfy in your special place, you are still breathing relaxed and easy. You begin to feel your mind and heart open and surrender to serenity. Let all your frustration, stress, and anxiety disappear with the peaceful energy surrounding you now. Let it go.

Now, with another deep breath, say within your mind *Let the past die. Let the past die. Let the past die.* Allow yourself to ponder these words. Allow images to form in your mind as this affirmation begins to direct you to past events, people, and emotions that you must let die so they no longer control you. The past is over, and it no longer controls you; let the hurtful situations and emotions connected with it die. The past dies because you are no longer giving these negative memories energy to feed on.

Take a full, cleansing breath and release any remaining negative residue with the exhale.

You are still breathing relaxed and easy. It's time now for the second affirmation. Say within your mind *Let the future unfold. Let the future unfold. Let the future unfold.* Allow the power of these words to direct your mind and heart to a positive outlook on your life. You have a future filled with love, abundance, and truth. Envision now the future you want to create, and feel it fall into place. Surrender to your future with ease and grace. Let the future unfold, and place it in the hands of divine faith. Still breathing relaxed and easy, say to yourself one more time, *let the future unfold.*

Take a deep cleansing breath and let out any remaining emotional fearful residue. Let it go.

Now, as you can still see within your mind, you are safe and relaxed in your special place. You begin to sense a vibrant energy surrounding you like a warm blanket. A sense of quiet security begins to well up within you. The healing taking place is opening up more channels of positive power in your life. The more you let go, the more you are free. You have a wonderful sense of your own personal power.

Now it's time for the third and final affirmation. Take a deep breath, and with the exhale say *Live in the present moment. Live in the present moment. Live in the present moment.* See your mind, body, spirit, and emotions all take charge as this affirmation directs them to fully integrate with each other into balanced, total harmony. There is peace in the now, there is life in the now, and the divine being is in the now. The divine is in the present moment with you, right here, right now. Live in the present moment. The only time is now.

As you take another deep breath and exhale, you feel all the affirmations begin to metabolize within your very being, as you say, *Let the past die; let the future unfold; live in the present moment.* An alchemical reaction is now taking place that will enrich your life from here on. Let the past die; let the future unfold; live in the present moment. This formula is the foundation for living a full and happy life.

Now, bring your attention to the top of your head. Visualize a bright sphere of white light hovering just a few inches above your head. The rays warm your forehead and shoulders. The light now begins to move down into the top of your head, past your forehead, through your throat, deep into your chest, past your stomach, into your sexual organs, and finally grounds itself at the base of your spine. Your entire body has been touched by the Holy Spirit, and now you are grounded in its presence.

Take a breath and feel yourself coming back into your body. You leave your special place and know that you can come back to it anytime you wish. Bring your attention to your body and begin to move around. You are feeling not only relaxed, but also grounded and vibrant with a new sense of life and your personal spiritual path. Open your eyes, take another deep breath, and with the exhale know that you can now fully engage in the mystical life you were born to live.

Oneness Prayer

Divine Spirit, I live your presence every day. You speak to my heart, and whispers of wisdom fill my soul. I'm here now because I'm enveloped in the present, where your spirit moves me. Help me to clear the past and release the future so that your presence and your voice are all I feel and hear. I'm here now, with you, and all is well. I am safe and protected. Your Holy Spirit touches me, and your divine hand safely guides me home, to the heart of my very soul. Divine Sprit, I thank you.

Wisdom Tips for Oneness

1. Again, take time to commune with nature. Nothing puts you in the now more than visually experiencing the ebb and flow of nature's cycles.

2. Keep setting aside personal quiet time with God. The more you go within, the more you become accustomed to the energy of the present and the divine presence within you.

3. Have animals in your life. Pets create a powerful state of unconditional love. They will always remind you of the power of now; that's all they know. See how happy they are because of Oneness consciousness? We can take a *re-minder* from our furry friends.

4. Let the past die; let the future unfold; live in the present moment. Use this formula and repeat it in your mind when times (pun intended) get tough.

CONCLUSION

THE JOURNEY CONTINUES

*I*t's my hope that the teachings in this book have helped and will continue to help you develop a stronger spiritual connection with your soul. I know that my journey, so far, has always led me back to the truth that the only journey worth taking is the journey within. When you get right down to it, what else is there in life but our soul's journey to its destiny? We may become distracted by the busy hustle and bustle of the physical plane, but nothing will ever be as secure as the sacredness of spirit that lies within. Continually *re-mind* yourself of that.

I want every one of my readers and students to know that within them is a strand of cosmic thread that is sacred and essential to the divine tapestry made up of all of life. Its sacred energy is vibrating all around us and within us. We, one by one, make a sacred connection that brings us closer to the realization that God is alive and well within each of us. Let that be your inner spark that wakes you every morning and that guides you to sleep every night. We are all one within the universal mind of God.

Acknowledgments

I'd like to thank Georgia Hughes and Kristen Cashman of New World Library for their support and the remarkable vision they gave for this work. Without it, *Reader of Hearts* would have been shelved! Special thanks and love to Kim Corbin, my publicist at New World Library. Skip on, girl!

Many blessings go to everyone at Findhorn Press for their input and support.

Much love to my dear friend Carol Johnson, my right hand and my right arm, my Carol! Thanks for everything you do to make me look less crazy.

To Mike May, my soul brother and friend, thank you for opening your heart and being there.

Thanks to Carol Simmons and Don Treadwell, my dear friends who have put up with me through thick and thin.

To Jane Olivor, thank you for not only your angelic voice and music that always touch my soul, but also your friendship and love. Your support and encouragement have gotten me through some rough times.

Much love to Joey Sheffield for your friendship and for putting up with my diva-ness!

Many thanks to Caroline Myss for your wisdom that has shed light on so many dark places in my life.

To Dolores Myss, much love and blessings for being my friend and "adopted" grandmother! I love you.

To my family, Mom, David, Angela, and Larry, thanks for your constant love and encouragement. I'm blessed to have been surrounded by all your beauty.

To Tom Strapp and everyone at Powersource for the creation of DarrinOwens.com. Your gifts of vision and creativity are unsurpassed.

Last, to all the friends, colleagues, and clients who have spread their magic in my life and made me stronger, of whom there are too many to name, I thank you. All of you are reflections of light; thank you for shining it my way.

To all of you, God bless.

RECOMMENDED RESOURCES

Books

Bodine, Echo. *A Still, Small Voice: A Psychic's Guide to Awakening Intuition*. Novato, CA: New World Library, 2001.

MacLaine, Shirley. *Out on a Limb*. New York: Bantam, 1986.

Moore, Thomas. *Dark Nights of the Soul: A Guide to Finding Your Way Through Life's Ordeals*. New York: Gotham, 2004.

Myss, Caroline, PhD. *Anatomy of the Spirit: The Seven Stages of Power and Healing*. New York: Three Rivers, 1997.

———. *Why People Don't Heal and How They Can*. New York: Three Rivers, 1998.

Powell, Robert. *The Sophia Teachings: The Emergence of the*

Divine Feminine in Our Time. New York: Lantern Books, 2001.

Puryear, Herbert B., PhD. *The Edgar Cayce Primer: Discovering the Path to Self-Transformation.* New York: Bantam, 1985.

Reed, Henry. *Edgar Cayce on Channeling Your Higher Self.* New York: Warner Books, 1989.

Tolle, Eckhart. *The Power of Now: A Guide to Spiritual Enlightenment.* Novato, CA: New World Library, 1999.

Wilde, Stuart. *The Three Keys to Self-Empowerment.* Carlsbad, CA: Hay House, 2004.

Audio

Williamson, Marianne. *Marianne Williamson on Self-Esteem.* New York: HarperAudio, 1992. Cassette.

———. *Spiritual Principles: Talks on Spirituality and Modern Life.* Carlsbad, CA: Hay House, 2004. 4 CDs.

———. *Mystical Power: Talks on Spirituality and Modern Life.* Carlsbad, CA: Hay House, 2004. 4 CDs.

Video

Higgins, Colin, and Shirley MacLaine. *Out on a Limb.* VHS. Directed by Robert Butler. New York: ABC Circle Films, 1987.

ABOUT THE AUTHOR

*D*arrin Owens has been a professional psychic and spiritual teacher for more than ten years. His speaking and teaching style is honest and lively, reflecting his early training as a professional singer. He travels throughout the United States offering private consultations as well as workshops on spirituality and developing spiritual abilities. He lives in Little Rock, Arkansas. Contact Darrin at:

DarrinOwens.com
P.O. Box 94341
North Little Rock, AR 72190

501-614-4655
www.darrinowens.com

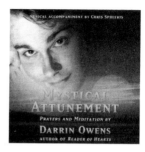

Mystical Attunement CD

by Darrin Owens (author of *Reader of Hearts*)

ISBN-10: 1-84409-047-7
ISBN-13: 978-1-84409-047-1

"Thank you for joining me. This is Darrin Owens, and I'm going to take you on a mystical journey. Together we will explore the inner landscapes that pave the way to becoming a mystic. I have designed this program to help you awaken a spiritual power, the power to live a mystical life.

"We all have an inner mystic just waiting for us to find it, claim it, and live it. A mystic has the privilege to see and experience God/Goddess in everything, including seeing that very sacredness within ourselves. This audio program will help you to do just that: attune to the essential, authentic part of you, the mystic.

"Each prayer is like an energetic download of spiritual wisdom. Think of them as seven invocations of the spirit. I'll explain each prayer before the actual invocations begin. At the end of the program, I'll leave you with a very powerful meditation that will skillfully direct you to let the past die, let the future create, and live in the present moment."

Contents, by track

1. Introduction to Prayers and Meditation
2. She, The Holy Spirit
3. Mystical Awakening: Attaining Insight
4. Mystical Darkness: Achieving Surrender
5. Mystical Power: Achieving Activation
6. Mystical Attunement: Achieving Connection
7. Mystical Co-Creation: Attaining Creativity
8. Mystical Living: Achieving Expression
9. Mystical Being Meditation: Activating the Power of Detachment

Available from your local bookstore
or directly from the publisher, www.findhornpress.com.

For a complete Findhorn Press catalogue,
please contact:

Findhorn Press
305a The Park, Findhorn
Forres IV36 3TE
Scotland, UK
tel 01309 690582
fax 01309 690036
info@findhornpress.com
www.findhornpress.com